THE NRI GUIDE

Information & Guide for Non-Resident Indians

V. K. Chand

THE NRI GUIDE

V. K. CHAND

Printed in USA

Dedication

In memory of my parents.

Parmeshwari Devi - Major Prithmi Chand Chadha.

♥

I can't seem to find words

to say how much I miss you!

Disclaimer

The opinions expressed in this book are those of the author and are not meant to be construed as professional advice of any kind. Information provided is based exclusively on my assessment of the subject matter and is not intended to offer legal, financial, immigration or professional counseling on any subject.

This book has been compiled from information available by way of various government notifications, government websites such as consulates, RBI, SEBI and sources such as taxation & customs documents/circulars available to the general public.

Laws, rules, policies and procedures do change periodically. Readers are urged to independently confirm from appropriate authorities or seek professional help before acting on any information provided in this book. In case of any variation between what has been stated in this book and the relevant Act, Rules, Regulations, Policy Statements etc. the latter shall prevail.

Although the author and publisher have made every effort to ensure that the information in this book was correct at press time, the author and publisher do not assume and hereby disclaim all liability to any party for loss, damage, or disruption caused by errors or omissions, whether such errors or omissions result from negligence, accident, or any other cause.

◆◆◆

About this book

This book is intended to help non-resident Indians understand some of the policies and procedures that they may have to deal with, because of their non-resident status in India.

The purpose of this book is to act as a reference guide and provide information on issues related to persons of Indian origin who are settled abroad. NRIs, OCI holders and foreign nationals of Indian origin, who continue to have close ties with India, will find helpful information in this book on various issues.

Persons of Indian origin who are contemplating relocating to India as the Indian economy picks up, will find information on topics such as, customs duties, setting up a business in India, taxation, banking, inheritance, repatriation, schools and more.

Readers should find procedures explained in a simple point by point format for the average reader to easily understand. Examples of different scenarios have been given to clarify, government rules and regulations effecting non-residents.

Whether you want to travel to India to visit relatives, buy a house in India, invest in agricultural land, start a new industrial venture or transfer money abroad from India, this book can help point you in the right direction.

While every effort has been made to provide up to date information, this book is not meant to replace professional advice. Readers are strongly advised to use professional guidance, especially when investing in India and clarify with the Indian consulates on visa related matters.

Table of Contents

Misperception on NRI definition

As the Indian tax system is based on residency, therefore it is important to understand the residential status of a person. Let's start with the definition of who is actually classified as a non-resident Indian (NRI).

One of the common misconceptions that I often come across is the meaning of non-resident Indian (NRI). For example, when the news media reports that NRIs may be allowed to vote in Indian elections, some non-resident Indians who live abroad and have acquired foreign citizenship, may assume that they might soon get the right to vote in Indian elections. This is a typical scenario where people fail to understand what NRI means.

A large majority of people generally define a non-resident Indian (NRI), as any former Indian citizen who moves out of India to live abroad. While this may be true to some extent, there are two types of NRI classifications.

1. Non-resident Indian (NRI)
2. Person of Indian origin (PIO)

The rules and regulations that a person falls under are based on such classifications. For example, the tax liability of a person would be based on the status of their residency classification.

Generally there are two categories of non-resident Indians, one is a citizen of India who is not living in India and is referred to as NRI. The other is a former citizen of India living abroad; such a person is classified as PIO, a person of Indian origin.

1. An Indian citizen, who holds an Indian passport and lives

abroad due to their work, studies etc. is an NRI.
Example: A person holding an Indian passport living in the United States on the basis of a 'Green Card'.

2. A former Indian citizen who acquires foreign citizenship is generally also referred to as a NRI, but in reality should be referred to as a person of Indian origin (PIO).

Referring to the vote example mentioned above, in the event the Indian government allows NRIs to vote in future, the NRI described in the first category would be able to vote. The PIO would not. Even though a PIO is a person of Indian origin, they are actually foreign citizens.

The example of NRI voting is used simply to highlight the NRI & PIO difference. For those who are interested, as of 2015 NRIs can vote in Indian elections.

While a person who is an NRI, may be allowed to do certain things according to Indian law, it is not necessary that a PIO would enjoy the same privileges, unless this is clearly stated by the Government of India.

Who is considered to be a person of Indian origin (PIO)

The most common definition of a person of Indian origin comes from the Foreign Exchange Management (Deposit) Regulations, 2000. You are deemed to be a person of Indian origin, if you are a foreign citizen (other than of Pakistan or Bangladesh), and if:

- You have at any time held an Indian passport.
- You or either of your parents or any of your grandparents were citizens of India by virtue of the Constitution of India

or the Citizenship Act, 1955

- You are the spouse of an Indian citizen or of a person of Indian origin (other than of Pakistan or Bangladesh)

The question of a person's origin, residence and citizenship normally arises in regard to seeking services or fulfilling legal obligations such as, complying with taxation rules etc.

Status of OCI holder living in India

OCI holders living in India continue to be classified as foreigners of Indian origin. OCI provides them with a lifetime Indian visa but they remain foreign citizens. They should continue to keep their foreign passport validity updated through the appropriate consulates of their home countries. OCI holders living in India do not automatically become India citizens after staying in India for five years or more. To get Indian citizenship, OCI holders must apply after completing the applicable residency requirements.

Foreign spouse of Indian citizen – Banking

For banking purposes, a foreign spouse of an Indian citizen is treated as a person of Indian origin provided they are not citizens of Pakistan or Bangladesh.

Foreign spouse of Indian citizen – Property Investment

For investment in real-estate purposes, a foreign spouse of an Indian citizen is also treated as a person of Indian origin, provided they are not citizens of Afghanistan, Bangladesh, Bhutan, Pakistan, Sri Lanka or Nepal.

Who is considered to be a person resident in India?

The determination of residency status in India is one of the most important aspects that affect foreign citizens. Regardless of what countries citizenship a person holds, a person can be deemed to be a resident of India in some circumstances.

Two conditions are considered to determine a person's resident status in India.

1. Length of stay in India. As per 'Foreign Exchange Management Act, 1999' (FEMA) a person is defined as a resident if they are in India for more than 183 days during the course of the previous financial year. The financial year in India is considered to be April 1st to March 31st.
2. Purpose of stay in India.

Residential status in India

The residential status of a persons is important when it comes to matters such as determining the tax liability. For Indian income tax purposes, a person can be:

1. Resident and ordinarily resident in India (ROR)
2. Non-resident (NR)
3. Resident but not ordinarily resident in India (RNOR)

The residential status of a person is decided under two different Acts:

1. Under Income Tax Act, 1961, (IT Act) and
2. Under Foreign Exchange Management Act (FEMA), 1999

What is Income Tax Act 1961?

The Income tax act 1961, governs the rules and regulations related to taxation in India. Comprehensive information on this act is available from 'Department of Revenue, Ministry of Finance' website: http://www.incometaxindia.gov.in/

What is FERA?

NRIs frequently hear the words FERA and FEMA when it comes to dealings that involve India in connection to foreign exchange transactions. Here is a brief summarized description of what FERA and FEMA mean.

The Foreign Exchange Regulation Act (FERA) is legislation that was passed by the Indian Parliament in 1973 and came into effect as of January 1, 1974. FERA imposed strict regulations on transactions involving foreign exchange and controlled the import and export of currency.

NRIs may perhaps remember a period, several years back, when there was a black market for buying and selling foreign currency in India. Eventually the government realized that FERA rules were perhaps a hindrance to economic liberalization.

FERA was repealed by the government in 1999 and replaced by the Foreign Exchange Management Act (FEMA), which liberalized foreign exchange controls and removed many restrictions on foreign investment. FEMA has emerged as an investor friendly legislation.

♦♦♦

What is the Foreign Exchange Management Act

FEMA came into effect on the 1st of June, 2000, replacing the Foreign Exchange Regulation Act (FERA).

The intentions of the Foreign Exchange Management Act are to perhaps, revise and unite laws that relate to transactions of foreign exchange and encourage an orderly maintenance and development, of the foreign exchange markets in India. FEMA is not as restrictive as some of the FERA regulations, and in line with India's economic liberalization policies.

Who is considered to be Non-Resident

The concept of Non-Resident under FERA is different as compared to that under Income Tax Act.

- Under Income Tax Act, the residential status of a person is determined on the basis of the number of days they stay in India.
- Under FERA, it is the intention of a person to be in India or outside India that is considered, as an important factor in determining their residential status. For example, a person may be India for only a short duration with the intention of employment.

Acquiring foreign citizenship

NRIs residing abroad, at some point of time have to make a decision as to whether they should acquire foreign citizenship. Such a decision would have been a lot easier, if India allowed dual citizenship, but this is not the case.

NRIs who acquire foreign citizenship now, have to formally renounce their Indian citizenship. Carefully considering the pros and cons of such a decision are important.

My website, nriinformation.com has on occasion received inquiries from persons of Indian origin, who want to know how to revert back and acquire Indian citizenship. In such cases, circumstances have changed for them and they feel it would be more advantageous for them to reclaim their Indian citizenship.

There is no definite answer on whether an NRI should or should not acquire foreign citizenship as each person's circumstances and future planning is unique. We can however, look at a few advantages and disadvantages of changing citizenship. Let us consider the disadvantages first.

Disadvantage of acquiring foreign citizenship

As far as disadvantages of acquiring foreign citizenship are concerned, here are some points to consider:

- Deep down, many NRIs perhaps have a feeling that they may eventually return to India for resettlement, hence they may worry about losing their Indian citizenship rights, if they choose to become foreign citizens.
- Some may be concerned about losing property they own in India, or may have worries of having to pay taxes on their worldwide income in two countries.
- Parents may have concerns that in case they eventually return to India, their children would be treated as foreigners by educational institutions. They might have to pay additional schooling fees.

Effects of renouncing Indian citizenship

On acquiring foreign citizenship, you may have to adjust to some changes that occur, when you give up Indian nationality.

Consider the following:

- For starters, you will have to renounce your Indian citizenship. Formal renunciation of Indian citizenship is now required from all Indian citizens who acquire foreign citizenship. This is a new rule that the Indian government announced in 2010. Currently without proof of formal renunciation of Indian citizenship, consular services at Indian consulates such as visas etc. cannot be availed.
- Once you acquire foreign citizenship, a visa is required if you wish to travel to India.
- For those who care, you lose your voting right in India.
- Travel to restricted areas in India, will also require a 'Restricted Area Permit' or 'Protected Area Permit'.
- Registration with Foreigner Regional Registration Office (FRRO) may be required, depending on the type of Indian visa and duration of stay in India during visits.

Changing citizenship is not merely a change of a passport but a decision that should be taken diligently.

Regardless of what route one takes, there will always be some form of adjustment required. Overall, this has to be a personal decision.

♦♦♦

Renunciation of citizenship affects your minor children

When an Indian citizen acquires foreign citizenship, they automatically lose their Indian citizenship. Under recent rules, a formal renunciation of Indian citizenship is required by anyone who acquires foreign citizenship.

Furthermore, when an individual renounces their Indian citizenship, their minor children automatically lose their Indian citizenship. The Indian nationality law follows the citizenship by 'right of blood' as opposed to citizenship by 'right of birth' within the territory.

Renunciation is covered in Section 8 of the Citizenship Act 1955. If an adult makes a declaration of renunciation of Indian citizenship, they lose their Indian citizenship. In addition, any minor child of that person also loses Indian citizenship from the date of renunciation.

When the child reaches the age of eighteen, he/she has the right to resume Indian citizenship. The provisions for making a declaration of renunciation under Indian citizenship law require that the person making the declaration be "of full age and capacity."

Sections 8, 'Renunciation of citizenship' parts which apply are reproduced below to provide further clarification.

1. If any citizen of India of full age and capacity, makes in the prescribed manner a declaration renouncing his Indian citizenship, the declaration shall be registered by the prescribed authority; and upon such registration, that person shall cease to be a citizen of India.

Where a person ceases to be a citizen of India under sub-section (1) every minor child of that person shall thereupon cease to be a citizen of India: Provided that any such child may, within one year after attaining full age, make a declaration (in the prescribed form and manner) that he wishes to resume Indian citizenship and shall thereupon again become a citizen of India.

Minor child loss of citizenship

If one parent renounces Indian citizenship will his/her minor children also automatically lose their Indian citizenship?

The requirement to renounce Indian citizenship after acquiring foreign citizenship came as a surprise to many former Indian citizens living abroad.

The rule in Section 8 of The Citizenship Act, 1955 dealing with loss of citizenship of minor children perhaps made sense when a person voluntarily renounced their Indian citizenship. This was something that rarely happened.

Now with the compulsory renunciation rule on acquiring foreign citizenship, thousands of individuals have no choice but to renounce their Indian citizenship and the effect of a parent's renunciation of citizenship on their minor children perhaps does not make sense.

I doubt if such a rule would be easy to apply especially in a case where only one parent renounces Indian citizenship! Perhaps the concerned authorities need to review this part of the Citizenship Act.

Advantages of acquiring foreign citizenship for NRIs

There may be certain benefits, of acquiring citizenship of the country you have settled in abroad.

- Getting visas of foreign countries from India, is a time consuming and perhaps a costly affair. Once you acquire the rights of citizenship, of your adopted country you are free to come and go without a visa.
- In some countries, for instance Canada, only citizens are allowed to work for the federal government. Acquiring Canadian citizenship opens up job opportunities with the Government of Canada. In the United States, only U.S. citizens and nationals may be appointed in the competitive civil services.
- Some countries provide medical and pension facilities that may be available only to their citizens.
- Citizens can come and go as often as they please. On the other hand, permanent residents of some countries, who are non-citizens, are restricted from leaving the country for longer periods and need to abide by the residency requirements, to keep their resident visas valid.
- Those who are not citizens may require a re-entry permit to enable them to return to the country after a prolonged absence, or risk having their residency visas being cancelled.

For example: *A green card holder in the United States may risk losing their 'Green Card' if on return to the United*

States, after an extended visit aboard, the visa officer feels that the person had abandoned residency.

A Canadian PR card holder would also be in the same situation if they stayed away for a prolonged period of time. Under current rules they must live in Canada for at least two years within a five year period.

Dual Citizenship - OCI

Persons of Indian origin settled abroad, have persistently demanded dual nationality for several years from the Indian government. However, as the Constitution of India, does not allow holding Indian citizenship and citizenship of a foreign country at the same time. Dual citizenship has not been awarded to former Indian citizens.

After repeated demands from persons of Indian origin, the Government of India on 2.12.2005 announced the start of the Overseas Citizen of India scheme (OCI).

By virtue of the Citizenship Act 1955, section 7A, foreign citizens who met the guidelines of being deemed to be of Indian origin, where allowed to register as 'Overseas Citizens of India'. This is commonly referred to by some people as dual citizenship. However OCI is not dual citizenship of India. Registration as an OCI provides the registrant, with an Indian visa for life, and some other specified benefits.

Citizenship Act, 1955 Section 7A (Extract from the Citizenship Act, 1955)
7A. Registration of overseas citizens of India.- The Central Government may, subject to such conditions and restrictions as may be prescribed, on an application made in this behalf, register as an overseas citizen of India- (a) any person of full age and capacity,-

(i) who is citizen of another country, but was a citizen of India at the time of, or at any time after, the commencement of the Constitution; or

(ii) who is citizen of another country, but was eligible to become a citizen of India at the time of the commencement of the Constitution; or

(iii) who is citizen of another country, but belonged to a territory that become part of India after the 15th day of August, 1947; or

(iv) who is a child or a grand-child of such a citizen; or

(b) a person, who is a minor child of a person mentioned in clause (a):

Provided that no person, who is or had been a citizen of Pakistan, Bangladesh or such other country as the Central Government may, by notification in the Official Gazette, specify, shall be eligible for registration as an overseas citizen of India.

OCI is not dual citizenship

There was initially some confusion created when OCI was announced. Some people assumed that OCI meant that they would be able to become dual citizens, get Indian citizenship and an Indian passport.

OCI however, did not mean dual citizenship but allowed the benefit of visa free, lifetime travel to India, along with certain benefits by which OCI holders would be treated at par, with other non-resident Indian citizens in economic, financial and educational fields.

Persons registered as OCI are not given Indian passports. OCI holders are given a passport like booklet that may look like a passport, but is basically a ceremonial document. OCI booklet is proof of OCI registration and should not be considered to be a document that can be used to travel with in lieu of a passport. Both OCI booklet and passport are required to travel to India.

Requirement to carry original passport with OCI relaxed

Previously there was a requirement that those travelling to India must have their foreign passport on which the original OCI 'U' visa was stamped with them or they could be denied entry. However, as of January 29, 2015 this rule was discontinued by the government of India. Now OCI holders can simply carry their OCI booklet as proof of their OCI status.

Kindly note, the OCI booklet is not a travel passport but is acceptable proof of OCI status. A valid passport is required to enter/exit India.

The Indian government has clarified, via announcements and notices on their consulate websites, that OCI should not be confused as Indian citizenship. Some people however, still seem to think of OCI as dual citizenship.

To clarify:

Example: Raj is a U.S. citizen and acquires an OCI card; he will not become a citizen of India. Raj will remain a citizen of the United States.

An OCI card is similar to a U.S. 'green card' or a Canadian PR card. OCI holders can travel to and from India indefinitely, work in India, study in India, and own property in India (except for certain agricultural and plantation properties). OCI holders, however, do not receive an Indian passport, cannot vote in Indian elections, and are not permitted to work in any capacity for the government of India.

While dual citizenship may probably have been the ideal

solution for many NRIs settled abroad. Overseas Citizen of India (OCI) is perhaps the best alternative for many foreign citizens of Indian origin.

The government of India has announced various benefits that can be availed by OCI holders. Some of the many benefits that are applicable to OCI registrants are listed below.

Kindly note:

The Ministry of Overseas Indian Affairs (MOIA) may from time to time announce other benefits for OCI holders under Section 7B (1) of the Citizenship Act, 1955.

Benefits allowed to OCI holders

Per section 7B of the Citizenship act

- Multi-purpose, multiple entries, lifelong visa for visiting India.
- Exemption from registration with local police authority for any length of stay in India.
- Parity with NRIs in respect of economic, financial and education fields, except in matters relating to the acquisition of agricultural/plantation properties.
- Parity with non-resident Indians on inter-country adoption.
- Parity with resident Indian nationals in domestic airfares
- Parity with Indian nationals in entry fees for national parks and wildlife sanctuaries
- Pursuing professions in India in pursuance of the provisions contained in the relevant act.

Professions such as:

- Doctors, Dentists, Nurses
- Pharmacists
- Advocates
- Architects
- Chartered Accountants

- Appear for the All India Pre-Medical Test or such other tests to make them eligible for admission in pursuance of the provisions contained in the relevant Acts.

- The Government of India has directed that: "State Governments should ensure that the OCI registration booklets of OCI are treated as their identification for any services rendered to them.

  In case proof of residence is required, Overseas Citizens of India may give an affidavit attested by a notary public stating that a particular/specific address may be treated as their place of residence in India and may also in their affidavit give their overseas residential address as well as email address, if any" [http://www.boi.gov.in]

- Any further benefits that may be announced by the Ministry of Overseas Indian Affairs (MOIA) under section 7B (1) of the Citizenship Act, 1955.

Restrictions on OCI holders

- ✓ Persons registered as OCI have not been given any voting rights; they are not allowed to stand for election to Lok Sabha, Rajya Sabha, and Legislative Assembly/Council.
- ✓ They cannot hold constitutional posts such as President, Vice President, and Judge of Supreme Court/High Court etc.

✓ OCI card holders cannot purchase agricultural or farm lands.

Extract Section 7B of the Citizenship act:

7B. Conferment of rights on overseas citizens of India.

(1)Notwithstanding anything contained in any other law for the time being in force, an overseas citizen of India shall be entitled to such rights other than the rights specified under sub-section(2) as the Central Government may, by notification in the Official Gazette, specify in this behalf.

(2) An overseas citizen of India shall not be entitled to the rights conferred on a citizen of India-

(a) under article 16 of the Constitution with regard to equality of opportunity in matters of public employment;

(b) under article 58 of the Constitution for election as President;

(c) under article 66 of the Constitution for election of Vice-President;

(d) under article 124 of the Constitution for appointment as a Judge of the Supreme Court;

(e) under article 217 of the Constitution for appointment as a Judge of the High Court;

(f) under section 16 of the Representation of the People Act, 1950(43 of 1950) in regard to registration as a voter;

(g) under sections 3 and 4 of the Representation of the People Act, 1951 (43 of 1951) with regard to the eligibility for being a member of the House of the People or of the Council of States, as the case may be;

(h) under section 5, 5A and 6 of the Representation of the People Act, 1951 (43 of 1951) with regard to the eligibility for being a member of the Legislative Assembly or a Legislative Council, as the case may be, of a State;

(i) for appointment to public services and posts in connection with the affairs of the Union or of any State except for appointment in such services and posts as the Central Government may by special order in that behalf specify.

(3) Every notification issued under sub-section (1) shall be laid before each House of Parliament.

Eligibility criteria for OCI

Foreign nationals, who wish to register themselves as overseas citizens of India are eligible if they:

- Were eligible to become a citizen of India on 6.01.1950, **or**
- Were a citizen of India on or at any time after 26.01.1950 **or**
- Belonged to a territory that became part of India after 15.08.1947
- Person of Indian Origin (PIO) card holders can also apply for OCI. Since the PIO card scheme has been cancelled by the Government of India.

Those who already have PIO cards can get OCI in lieu of their PIO card free of cost. The cutoff date for accepting application for OCI registration in lieu of PIO card is March 31, 2016.

PIO card holders do not get OCI automatically, they must apply for it.

- In addition to meeting the eligibility requirement for registration as an OCI, the applicant's country of citizenship should also allow dual citizenship in some form or under their local laws.
- Those who have ever been a citizen of Pakistan or Bangladesh are not eligible for registration as an Overseas Citizen of India.

Foreign spouse of Indian citizen - OCI

Previously a foreign spouse of an Indian citizen could not apply for OCI based exclusively on the fact that they were married to an Indian citizen. There was a requirement that to be eligible to apply for OCI, a foreign spouse must satisfy the eligibility requirements for OCI on their own capacity.

This rule was changed as of January 06, 2015. It is now easier for foreign spouses to get OCI registration. Under current rules:

Foreign spouse is eligible for OCI if:

- Spouse married to a Citizen of India and whose marriage has been registered and subsisted for a continuous period of not less than two years immediately preceding the presentation of the application under this section;

  Or
- A Spouse married to an Overseas Citizen of India cardholder registered under section 7A and whose marriage has been registered and subsisted for a continuous period of not less than two years immediately preceding the presentation of the application under this section.

OCI rules for foreign born children of Indian citizens

There are often cases where parents who are both Indian citizens, are living abroad due to employment etc. want to register their foreign born children as Overseas Citizens of India (OCI).

When it comes to minors, OCI rules, previously took into consideration the citizenship of the child's parents.

Prior to January 06, 2015, foreign born minor children (Less than 18 years), where farther and mother were both Indian Citizens, were not eligible for OCI. There was a requirement that at least one of the child's parents had to be a foreign citizen for a minor to be eligible to apply for OCI.

This rule does not apply now. As of January 06, 2015 minor children are eligible for OCI registration even if both parents are Indian citizens.

♦♦♦

Who is Not Eligible for OCI

- Former Bangladesh/Pakistan Nationals
- If your parents/grandparents/great grandparents have ever been a citizen of Pakistan or Bangladesh.
- In case of foreign spouse, if marriage has not been registered and/or subsisted for a continuous period of two years immediately preceding the presentation of the application under this section
- Foreign Spouse separated from Indian origin spouse
- If the Indian spouse has deceased

- Foreign military personnel (Armed Forces/Para-military/ security/Police/Intelligence, either in service or retired.
- Children of Foreign military personnel of Armed Forces/ Para-military/security/Police/Intelligence, either in service or retired
- Former citizens of Pakistan or Bangladesh are not eligible for OCI.
- Children of Parents/Grandparents/Great grandparents who are of Bangladesh/Pakistan Origin

Example: *A US Citizen of Indian origin is married to a girl who is a Pakistani national. While he is eligible to apply for OCI, his wife is not eligible.*

How to apply for OCI

Applications for registration as an Overseas Citizen of India (OCI) have to be made online form the designated government 'Online OCI Services' website: https://passport.gov.in/oci/

Applicants are required to fill and submit their online application and also mail in a printed copy of the application they submitted online with the required documentation to the applicable office for processing. In the near future, the requirement to send hard copy of OCI applications is expected to be eliminated and entire OCI application process moved online. This should make it easier for new OCI applicants.

OCI applications from abroad or India

The application process for OCI registration is the same whether the applicant is in India or abroad. The only difference being that the mailing in part of the application and documents are mailed to the appropriate Indian mission when applying from abroad and to the concerned FRRO when applicant is applying from within India.

OCI application is started by accessing the application form online from the Indian Government's website. Currently the website address is https://passport.gov.in/oci/
(Please note: The instructions provided can be changed by the authorities at their discretion. Generally the application form provides the latest procedure to fill and submit application.)

If you use a browser such as Firefox, Chrome or Safari, it is recommended that you use Internet Explorer when trying to access online application forms on Government of India websites. Using other browsers may sometimes lead unformatted pages.

The OCI application is in two parts: Part 'A' and Part 'B'. Part 'A' MUST be filled first online by the person applying for OCI. After Part-A has been completed and submitted online. Applicants are then directed to Part-B which should also be filled online. An ID number is generated on submission.

Print Part A and Part B as these forms along with the requisite documents have to be submitted by mail to the Indian mission or FRRO whichever is applicable depending on the location of the applicant.

To start your online application:

1. On the internet, visit:
   https://passport.gov.in/oci/

2. Select whether you are applying as an individual or as a

family. When you select the on-line registration form as "Family" option, then the on-line registration form will allow data entry for a family of up to four persons.

*Family Group option should be chosen only if one of the parents is applying along with one/two minor children or husband & wife are applying. Otherwise select the individual option. If there are more members in the family, or children are not minor, then their applications should be filed out as individuals.

3. The OCI application is in two parts: Part 'A' and Part 'B'. Part 'A' MUST be filled first online by the person applying for OCI. After Part-A has been completed and submitted online. Applicants are then directed to Part-B which should also be filled online. An ID number is generated on submission. Print Part A and Part B
4. The next step involves submission to the appropriate authority (depending on applicant's location) of the hard copy of the application forms the applicant printed along with the required documents and fee. A list of documents to be enclosed along with application are given at the end of Part-B.

Original Documents Requirement for OCI applicants

The documents submitted with OCI application are copies of original documents and self-attested by the applicant. No original documents are sent with the application. However, applicants will have to show the original documents for verification purpose at the time of collecting the OCI Card.

As rules and regulation, sometimes do change. Do read the instructions provided on your form before mailing out your application form and documents.

OCI fee for applications made abroad

OCI application fee, when the scheme was initially announced was US$275. While the fee has technically not been changed, many Indian consulates have outsourced visa services and fee charged by the outsourcing company is passed on to applicants.

The fee currently for OCI in USA is US$295 (this includes the outsourcing company charges). Fees are subject to change, kindly check with the appropriate Indian consulates for the required fee when applying for OCI.

Documents required with OCI application

1. Proof of present citizenship

2. Evidence of self or parents or grandparents,

- ✓ Being eligible to become a citizen of India at the time of Commencement of the Constitution;

  or

- ✓ Belonging to a territory that became a part of India after 15th August, 1947;

  or

- ✓ Being a citizen of India on or after 26th January, 1950.

These documents could be:

- ✓ Copy of the passport: **or**
- ✓ Copy of the domicile certificate issued by the Competent

Authority; **or**

- ✓ Evidence of relationship as parent/grandparent, if their Indian Origin is claimed as basis for grant of OCI.*

*If parents/grandparents origin is being claimed as basis for grant of OCI, the following documents are required:

- ➢ Those who are claiming OCI card on the basis of parent's Indian origin, their birth certificate showing their parents name is required.
- ➢ If you are claiming Indian origin based on your grandparents origin, then you have to submit your birth certificate as well as your parents' birth certificate showing the parents' names clearly so that it establishes the relation with your parents and grandparents.
- ➢ Copy of their Indian passport, or
- ➢ Copy of their domicile certificate issue by the competent authority; or any other documentary evidence like a notarized copy of school certificate, land ownership certificate by which eligibility can be logically established. Whether to accept the proof submitted would depend on the Consular Officer.

OCI - Foreign born children of Indian citizens

For minor children whose parents are citizens of India, the following documents are also required:

- ➢ A copy of the child's birth certificate
- ➢ Copies of Indian passport of Indian parents or a copy of Domicile or Nativity Certificate as proof that the parents are indeed Indian citizens

- If parents are divorced then a court order showing dissolution of marriage and proof of legal custody of the child with the parent who is applying for the child's OCI

OCI – Foreign origin spouse of Indian citizen

Where the OCI applicant is of foreign origin and spouse of an Indian citizen the following additional documents are required:

- Marriage certificate
- Passport copy of Indian spouse or a copy of Domicile or Nativity Certificate as proof that the spouse is an Indian citizen
- If spouse is an OCI card holder then a copy of the OCI card and passport is required

Any other proof, that is acceptable to the authorities as proof of the applicant being of Indian origin.

When it comes to accepting other types of proof as supporting documents, the final decision to accept any type of document as proof would rest with the consular officers. Some documents that might stand a chance of being accepted may be:

- Documentary evidence like a school certificate.
- Land ownership records in India.
- Birth certificate.
- Any other type of documentation whereby eligibility may be reasonably ascertained to the satisfaction of the Indian government official dealing with your application.

Surrender certificate requirement

Former Indian Nationals, who apply for OCI, are also required to provide a 'Surrender Certificate' to show they had renounced their Indian citizenship after they acquired foreign citizenship. Information regarding obtaining a surrender certificate is provide separately in this book.

OCI photo guidelines

One of the reasons for delay of processing OCI applications is the rejection of the photographs which are sent in by applicants, as they do not meet the acceptable format set by the authorities. Care should be taken that the photographs you are sending meet the required guidelines. Photo guidelines can be viewed by visiting:
http://passport.gov.in/oci/Photo-Spec-FINAL.pdf

Checking status of OCI application

Applicants can check the status of their OCI application on the internet. To check your application status, visit the OCI status check website at https://passport.gov.in/oci/

Approval of OCI application

The practice of pasting OCI 'U' visa sticker on passports of OCI holders is being discontinued. Once an applicant's OCI is approved, they will be given an OCI booklet as proof of their OCI registration. The OCI booklet will be proof of OCI status and accepted as proof when traveling to India.

OCI applications in India

As per Indian Citizenship Rules, 1956 (25C) Persons of Indian origin can also apply for OCI in India. Applications in India for OCI can be made to:

- The Foreigner's Regional Registration Officer (FRRO) **OR**
- The Chief Immigration Officer (CHIO) in Chennai **OR**
- OCI Cell in Foreigners Division of Ministry of Home Affairs at: Under Secretary (Foreigners Division)
  Ministry of Home Affairs, Jaisalmer House. 26 Man Singh Road, New Delhi – 110 011

OCI fee in India

For applications that are filed in India, the current fee is Rs 15,000/- for each applicant. The fee is paid in the form of a demand draft, payable at New Delhi and made in favor of Accounts Officer (Secretariat), Ministry of Home Affairs New Delhi.

OCI fee Refund

In a case where the OCI application is rejected, the fee paid is returned after deducting US$25 or equivalent that is charged as processing fee. All fees mentioned here, are subject to change by the authorities at their discretion.

OCI disadvantages for US citizens

There are occasionally concerns expressed by some prospective applicants, whether registration as an OCI can cause problems for U.S. citizens of Indian origin.

What concerns such American citizens of Indian origin is that:

1. They may have problems if their line of work requires them to have security clearance for accessing government information.
2. They may be passed over when it comes to promotions because of their OCI status. They somehow feel that they may project an image of not being truly American by wanting some sort of dual citizenship.

Are such concerns valid? It's difficult to say, taking into account the security concerns of countries worldwide. American citizens who are reluctant to apply for OCI previously had the option of applying for a "Person of Indian Origin" (PIO) card. However this option is no longer available as the PIO scheme was cancelled in 2015 by the government of India*
[vide Gazette Notification No.25024/9/2014F.I dated 09 January 2015]

Cancellation of OCI status

OCI status can be cancelled by the Government of India, in cases where false information was furnished or material information was suppressed. If registration as OCI has already been granted, it can be cancelled under section 7D of the Citizenship Act, 1955.

Cancellation of OCI registration by government

The Government of India can cancel OCI registration:

- If it is found that the registration as an OCI was obtained by means of fraud, false representation; **or**
- The concealment of any material fact; **or**

- The registered OCI has shown disaffection towards the Constitution of India or comes under any of the provisions of section 7D of the Citizenship Act.

The registration of such persons is not only cancelled, but the authorities may blacklist such persons, to prevent their future entry into India.

To offer more clarity on this topic, the exact wording from the Citizenship Act, 1955 Section 7D that deals with this topic is provided below.

Extract from Section 7D - Cancellation of Registration

7D. Cancellation of registration as overseas citizen of India.- The Central Government may, by order, cancel the registration granted under sub-section(1) of section 7A if it is satisfied that-

(a) the registration as an overseas citizen of India was obtained by means of fraud, false representation or the concealment of any material fact; or

(b) the overseas citizen of India has shown disaffection towards the Constitution of India as by law established; or

(c) the overseas citizen of India has, during any war in which India may be engaged, unlawfully traded or communicated with an enemy or been engaged in, or associated with, any business or commercial activity that was to his knowledge carried on in such manner as to assist an enemy in that war; or

(d) the overseas citizen of India has, within five years after registration under sub-section(1) of section 7A has been sentenced to imprisonment for a term of not less than two years; or

(e) it is necessary so to do in the interest of the sovereignty and integrity of India, the security of India, friendly relations of India with any foreign country, or in the interests of the general public.

♦♦♦

Renunciation of OCI

There is always a possibility that some OCI registrants may at some point of time decide to cancel their OCI registration for personal reasons. For instance, a US citizen may feel that their OCI registration may cause a problem when seeking security clearance for certain jobs associated with the US government.

Section 7C of the citizenship act provides guidelines for renunciation of OCI.

OCI registrants can declare their intention to renounce their OCI registration to the Indian Mission, where their OCI registration was originally granted. After receipt of the declaration, the Indian Mission/Consulate shall issue an acknowledgement in Form XXIIA.

The exact wording from the Citizenship Act, 1955 Section 7C that deals with 'Renunciation' is provided.

Extract from section 7C – Renunciation

7C. Renunciation of overseas citizenship.-
(1) If any overseas citizen of India of full age and capacity makes in the prescribed manner a declaration renouncing his overseas citizenship of India, the declaration shall be registered by the

Central Government, and; upon such registration, that person shall cease to be an overseas citizen of India.

(2) Where a person ceases to be an overseas citizen of India under subsection (1), every minor child of that person registered as an overseas citizen of India, shall thereupon cease to be an overseas citizen of India.

Sample of Renunciation Acknowledgement Form

FORM XXII A

(See rule 25 H)

Sample form XXIIA

ACKNOWLEDGEMENT

Received declaration of renunciation of Overseas Citizenship of India under section 7C (1) of the Citizenship Act, 1955 from Miss/Ms./Mr. . . . .
D/o, W/o,

S/o . . . . resident of

Date: . . . . Signature with seal of the Receiving Officer

Note: Strike out whichever is not applicable.

Renewal of OCI Requirement

While OCI provides a visa for a lifetime; to keep records in order, the OCI registration certificate and visa have to be re-issued in some cases.

Renewal of OCI is required:

1. Each time a new passport is issued up to the completion of 20 years of age. OCI documents have to be re-issued and payment of appropriate fee is required.
2. Once an OCI holder reaches age 50, they must get their OCI registration certificate and visa re-issued.

Between the ages of 21 and 50, there is no mandatory requirement to get documents re-issued

Requirement to carry original U Visa passport

OCI holders at some point of time replace their passports when their passport validity expires. When traveling to India, OCI holders who got new passports under previous rules were required to either get their OCI U visa stamped on the new passport or carry both; their expired passport with original U visa stamp and their new passport as proof of their OCI status. This rule no longer applies.

As of January 29, 2015 there is no requirement to carry your old passport having the original U visa. The OCI booklet will now be acceptable proof of OCI status.

In case someone wishes to get fresh documents issued to them as a matter of convenience, they can do so on payment of the appropriate fee.

Changes to OCI 'U' Visa Record

Those who are already registered as Overseas Citizens of India (OCI) and require changes to their OCI record can make some changes by using the OCI Miscellaneous Services. The link to their website is: https://passport.gov.in/oci/welcome

Using OCI Miscellaneous Services

OCI Miscellaneous Services can be used for re-issuance or issuance of duplicate OCI documents in the following cases:

- In case of issuance of new passport.
- In case of change of personal particulars viz. nationality etc.
- In case of loss/damage of OCI registration certificate/visa.
- In case of filling of wrong personal particulars while submitting online applications viz. name, father's name, date of birth etc.
- In case of manually filled in applications that were done earlier and had errors that were made by consular staff while entering personal particulars.
- In case change of address/occupation is required.

OCI Miscellaneous Services Online

OCI Miscellaneous Services can be availed by filling and submitting the required application online and sending one hard copy of the application form to the concerned Indian Mission/Post/Office in whose jurisdiction the applicant is resident.

Even if the OCI documents were issued elsewhere and you have moved to a new address, you can submit application to the Indian Mission that is applicable to your current location.

The fact that the OCI documents have not been issued from that Indian Mission/Consulate should not make a difference.

OCI Miscellaneous Services in India

Those who avail OCI Miscellaneous services in India are required to submit their application to:

- The Under Secretary, OCI Cell, Foreigners Division, Ministry of Home Affairs (MHA), Jaisalmer House, 26 Man Singh Road, New Delhi – 110 011

  OR
- To the concerned Foreigners Regional Registration Officer (FRRO) applicable to their area of residence. A list of FRRO offices in India is provided in this book.

How to use OCI Miscellaneous Services

To start using OCI Miscellaneous Services, first visit the Miscellaneous Services Website. The URL for their website is https://passport.gov.in/oci/ select 'Click Here To Proceed' and on the next page select '**OCI Miscellaneous_Services'** To get access to the services section, applicants are required to provide one of the following data fields:

- ✓ First, the applicant's Passport number has to be entered in the space provided on the online application form. This should be the same passport number shown on your 'U' visa stamp.
- ✓ Next, **one** of the following three fields will be required to be filled in to proceed:
    - U-Visa Number

      or
    - OCI Registration Number **or**
    - OCI File Number

- ✓ Next step requires **all** of the following three fields to be filled.
    - Date of birth
    - Place of birth
    - Mother's maiden name

Once this information is filled in, click the 'Submit' button.

If the information entered is correct, the applicant is then given access to the appropriate form, where they can select and make the desired changes. After the required changes have been made and verified, click the submit button again to transmit the data.

Upon submission of the 'Online Registration Form', a hard copy of the application with a Reference number, along with instructions for filling the application form are shown. After printing the form, applicant can paste a photograph on the space provided in the form, and sign in the appropriate box.

A copy of the signed application form, along with required documentation has to be mailed to the concerned Indian Mission, in your area. Instructions on the printed hard copy will advise how many copies to mail. Normally, two sets are requested.

The only exception to this is that when the changes entered are only a change in address or occupation, then no hard copy is required to be mailed in and for this type of change there is no fee payable.

♦♦♦

Fee for OCI Miscellaneous Services

For re-issuance of OCI documents, in case of:

- New passport
- Change of personal particulars
- To correct information that is currently wrong

The fee is US $ 25 or equivalent in local currency.

In case of applications that are filed in India, for the above services, the fee is Rs. 1400/- and is payable by demand draft in favor of 'Pay and Accounts Officer (Secretariat), Ministry of Home Affairs' payable at New Delhi.

- For issuance of duplicate OCI documents in case of loss or damage, the fee charged is US$ 100 or equivalent in local currency.
- In case application for duplicate OCI documents is filed in India, the fee is Rs. 5500/-

Please note

Fee mentioned above are current but are all subject to change at the discretion of the government of India. Kindly confirm with Indian consulates or FRRO.

Lost – Damaged OCI Documents

In case your foreign passport that has your OCI 'U' visa stamped on it is stolen or lost. You should report the loss to the local police in the area where the documents were lost. When you apply for new OCI documents in such cases, a copy of the police complaint you made regarding your loss, will be required.

Normally in cases where new OCI documents are requested due to loss of original documents, a personal interview with the consular official may also be required. Generally when you send your application in, you will be notified the date and time of the interview by the authorities.

Recording Address Changes on OCI

In case of change of address/occupation, simply log into OCI miscellaneous services website, make the required address or occupation change and you are done. There is also no fee for this type of change. When you initiate a change of address or occupation via miscellaneous services, new OCI documents are not issued.

Upon submission of online application, the data is recorded and new address/occupation can be printed and kept in the OCI registration certificate booklet for record purposes.

PIO Card Scheme Cancelled

The Person of Indian Origin Card (PIO CARD) was launched by the Government of India in 1999. The PIO card was intended to make it easier for foreign nationals of Indian origin, to enter India with ease and avoid the process of applying for visas every time they wanted to visit. As of January 9, 2015 the PIO card scheme has been withdrawn.

Lifetime Validity stamp for PIO card holders

On September 30, 2014 The Government of India published in the Gazette of India (Part-I, Section-I) that a PIO card issued to an applicant shall be valid for his/her lifetime, provided such applicant has a valid Passport.

PIO card holders who wish to get a Lifetime Validity stamp on their PIO card can do so by contacting the Indian consulate in their area of residence.

Those who are travelling can get lifelong stamp done on arrival or exit from India at the immigration counters. FRRO offices in India is another option for PIO card holders in India.

Travel to India with PIO Card

At the time of printing of this book, those who already hold PIO cards and have not yet opted for OCI in lieu of PIO, can still travel to Indian using their PIO card and valid foreign passport.

According to information available, 31st March 31, 2016 is supposed to be the last day for current PIO card holders to apply for OCI card in lieu of their PIO card.

♦♦♦

PIO Card Scheme Cancellation – Overview

On 09 January 2015 Government of India has notified that all the existing Persons of Indian Origin (PIO) card holders registered as such under the PIO Card scheme 2002, shall be deemed to be Overseas Citizens of India Cardholders (Merger of PIO & OCI Schemes).

Those who applied for PIO cards before the announcement of cancellation of PIO card scheme will have to apply for OCI as PIO applications will not be processed due to cancellation of PIO scheme.

Existing PIO Card holders can apply for OCI

Those who currently hold PIO cards can apply for an OCI card. Previously September 30, 2015 was announced as the last day for existing PIO card holders to apply for OCI. This date was later extended to 31st March 31, 2016. This date may or may not be extended again. Those who currently hold PIO cards will not automatically get OCI. They must apply for OCI if they wish to take advantage of the OCI in lieu of PIO card offer, announced by the government of India.

Currently there is no fee for applying for OCI in Lieu of PIO card. Service charges by companies contracted to provide services by Indian consulates may charge some type of service fee.

How to apply for OCI in Lieu of PIO Card

PIO holders can apply for OCI in lieu of PIO Card online by visiting http://passport.gov.in/oci/welcome or http://passport.gov.in/oci/capchaActionPIO

Points to remember

- PIO card of applicant must have been valid as on January 9, 2015 to get OCI in lieu of PIO Card
- Instructions on filling the form are provided on the first page. Read instructions carefully and save form before exiting, in case you wish to return to complete the form later
- There is no fee payment required for getting OCI in lieu of PIO Card. However, service charges of for the outsourcing company if any and postage charges will be charged.

Reminder

The last date for current PIO card holders to apply for OCI in lieu of PIO card is March 31, 2016. This date may or may not be extended by the government of India.

Citizenship in India

The Citizenship Act, 1955 deals with questions about Indian citizenship. It provides information on acquisition and determination of citizenship. The various modes of acquiring Indian citizenship are summarized in this chapter.

How to Acquire Indian Citizenship

Citizenship of India can be acquired by:

- Birth
- Descent
- Registration
- Naturalization
- Incorporation of territory

Here is a brief summary of each category:

Citizenship by birth

Every person born in India on or after January 26, 1950, but before July 1, 1987 is a citizen of India by birth. The nationality of their parents in such cases does not matter.

A person born in India on or after July 1, 1987, is considered a citizen of India only if at least one of the person's parents was a citizen of India at the time of birth. Furthermore, in cases where one parent is a citizen of India and the other is not, the other parent's status in India should be legal. *(Vide Citizenship Act 1955 Section 3)*

♦♦♦

Citizenship by Descent

A person born outside India on or after January 26, 1950 but before December 10, 1992 is a citizen of India by descent provided; his/her father was a citizen of India at the time of his birth.

Those born on or after December 10, 1992, are considered Indian citizens by descent, only if either of the person's parents, was a citizen of India at the time of birth and the birth was registered at an India consulate within the prescribed period. *(Vide Citizenship Act 1955 Section 4)*

Please note: Indian citizens residing abroad, who wish to apply for an Indian passport for their foreign born child; should NOT apply for a foreign passport for the child. In case they do get a foreign passport for their new born child, they cannot get an Indian passport for their child until the child reaches the age of majority and opts for Indian citizenship.

Under no circumstances can Indian citizens hold passports of two countries at the same time.

Citizenship by Registration

Citizenship by registration can be acquired by:

- Persons of Indian origin who have resided in India for at least seven years, before applying for citizenship.
- Persons who are or have been married to Indian citizens and are residing in India for seven years before applying for Indian citizenship. ***And***
  throughout the period of twelve months immediately

before making application,
And
for SIX YEARS in the aggregate in the EIGHT YEARS preceding the twelve months.

- Minor children of persons who are Indian citizens.

(As per Citizenship Act 1955 Section 5)

Citizenship by Naturalization

As per Citizenship Act 1955, Section 6, foreigners can acquire Indian citizenship by way of naturalization. Applications for citizenship by naturalization can be made by:

- Foreigners who have resided in India for ten years.
- They must have stayed in India continuously for at least one year preceding the date of their application for citizenship.
- In the past twelve years, they must have lived in India for at least nine years.

Citizenship by Incorporation of territory

Citizenship of India, by incorporation of territory applies when a territory becomes part of India. Persons of that territory are granted Indian citizenship by the Government of India from a specified date. *(As per Citizenship Act 1955 Section7)*

Extended Stay in India may not guarantee Citizenship

It should be noted that simply meeting the residency requirements, does not in any way guarantee that a person can claim Indian citizenship. In a scenario where a person visiting India, decides to simply start living in India without a valid visa.

Even though, such a person may successfully establish themselves as a resident in India, purchase a house, obtain a ration card and perhaps establish a successful business, they cannot hope to get Indian citizenship. If discovered by the authorities, such persons would be deported. Those who reside in India without legal status cannot apply for Indian citizenship, regardless of how long they have lived in India.

PIO/OCI Acquiring Indian Citizenship

Persons of Indian origin (PIO) and those registered as overseas citizens of India (OCI) can apply for Indian citizenship if they wish, once they have fulfilled the residency requirements.

Here is a brief explanation of each category and the residency requirements:

Person of Indian Origin (PIO) is usually a person of Indian origin who is not a citizen of India but was either an Indian citizen before acquiring foreign citizenship or whose ancestors were holding Indian citizenship.

- As per section 5(1) (a) & 5(1) (c) of the Citizenship Act, a person of Indian origin has to reside in India for minimum 7 years, before they can make an application for grant of Indian citizenship.

OCI is a person registered as Overseas Citizen of India (OCI) under section 7A of the Citizenship Act, 1955

- Registered OCI may be granted Indian citizenship after 5 years from date of registration. Earlier there was a condition that the applicant must have stayed in India for at least one year prior to making application. This rule has now amended as of January 6, 2015. The current rule states:

'Provided that if the Central Government is satisfied that special circumstances exist, it may, after recording the circumstances in writing, **relax the period of twelve months** up to a maximum of thirty days which may be in different breaks.'

Loss of Indian Citizenship

The Indian government, as per section 10 of the Indian Citizenship Act, 1955, may withdraw Indian citizenship from any person if they are satisfied that:

- The registration or certificate of naturalization was obtained by means of fraud, false representation or the concealment of any material fact; **or**
- that citizen has shown himself by act or speech to be disloyal or disaffected towards the Constitution of India as by law established; **or**
- that citizen has, during any war in which India may be engaged, unlawfully traded or communicated with an enemy or been engaged, in or associated with any business that was to his knowledge carried on in such manner as to assist and enemy in that war; **or**
- That citizen has, within five years after registration or naturalization, been sentenced in any country to imprisonment for a term of not less than two years; **or**

- that citizen has been ordinarily resident out of India for a continuous period of seven years, and during that period, has neither been at any time a student of any educational institution in a country outside India or in the service of the Government in India or of an international organization of which India is a member, nor registered annually in the prescribed manner at an Indian consulate his intention to retain his citizenship of India.

Birth Registration at Indian Consulate

Indian citizens, who reside abroad, can register the birth of their new born child at Indian consulates in the country where they reside. In such cases, an Indian passport for the child can also be obtained, provided the child has not obtained a passport of the country of birth.

Advantages of registering birth

Indian citizens residing abroad should register their new born children at the nearest Indian consulates. Suppose, Indian parents who are residing in the United States due to employment, give birth to a baby in USA, the child would be a US citizen by birth. If parents register the birth at the Indian consulate, their child will have the option of claiming Indian citizenship when reaching the age of majority.

In such a case, parents would also have the option of applying for an Indian passport for their foreign born child. However, if they chose this route, they must not apply for a US passport for their new born.

Documents required for birth registration

Along with the application for birth registration, the following documents are required.

- A copy of the birth certificate of the child.
- A copy of the passport of both the parents.
- A copy of the certificate of Indian citizenship if acquired by registration/naturalization.
- A copy of the marriage certificate of the parents.

Foreigners Regional Registration Office Guide

Foreigners' registration work in India is handled by the Bureau of Immigration. The officers in charge of immigration and registration activities of foreigners, are called Foreigners Regional Registration Officers. Foreigners Regional Registration Offices (FRRO) are located in major cities of India. They have offices in:

- Ahmedabad
- Amritsar
- Bangalore
- Calicut
- Chennai
- Cochin
- Delhi
- Goa
- Hyderabad
- Kolkata
- Lucknow
- Mumbai
- Trivandrum

In cities across India where there are no FRRO offices, the concerned 'District Superintendents of Police' function as Foreigners Registration Officers. When there is a requirement to register at the FRRO and no FRRO office is in the city you are in, the office of the District Superintendent of Police should be contacted.

Services at FRRO Offices

Generally the following services are preformed:

- Visa Extensions: Tourist visas are generally non-extendable; however in cases of persons of Indian origin, after submission of relevant documents to the satisfaction of the authorities, tourist visa may be extended.

- Issue exit visas.
- Registration of foreigners in India as per their visa requirements.
- Accept OCI applications at their offices.

Checklist for Registration Formalities at FRRO

All foreigners visiting India, who have visas for a period exceeding 6 months duration, are required to get themselves registered within 14 days of their arrival at the nearest office of the FRRO. Those who have PIO cards or OCI, are exempt from the registration requirement.

The type of documents one would require would depend on the type of service being sought from the FRRO. A list of the type of documents that are generally required is provided here:

- Original passport on which visa is endorsed.
- Photocopy of the passport and initial visa.
- Four photographs of the applicant.
- Details of residence in India.
- Those who are visiting India on a long term visa of more than one year and are in the age group of 15 to 60 years. Require a HIV test report, from one of the WHO recognized Institutions.
- Copy of the marriage certificate, in case of those seeking extension of stay on grounds of being the spouse of an Indian national.
- Certificate from the University, College, or Institution in

case of Student visa.

- Accreditation certificate from Press Information Bureau in case of Journalist visa.
- Approval of the Department of Company Affairs in case of Board level appointments in Public Limited Companies.
- Copy of the approval from Government of India in case of a joint venture or collaboration.
- Copy of permission from the RBI in case of contract or agreement, in case of business/joint ventures etc.
- Terms and conditions of appointment and copy of contract or agreement, in case of Employment visa.
- An undertaking from the concerned Indian company in case of Employment/Business visas.

FRRO Office Locations in India:	
Delhi	East Block-VIII, Level-II, Sector-1, R.K. Puram, New Delhi-110066 Telephone No: 011-26711384 Fax: 011-26711348 Email ID: frrodli@nic.in
Mumbai	3rd floor, Special Branch Building, Badruddin Tayabji Lane, Mumbai-400001 Telephone No.022-22621169 Fax: 022-22620721 Email ID frromum@nic.in
Chennai	Shastri Bhawan, 26, Haddows Road, Chennai-600006 Telephone No: 044-23454970 Fax: 044-23454971 Email ID: frrochn@nic.in
Kolkata	237, Acharya Jagdish Chandra Bose, Road, Kolkata-700020 Telephone No: 033-224700549 - Fax: 033-22470549 Email ID: frrokol@nic.in
Amritsar	123-D, Ranjit Avenue, Amritsar-143001 Telephone No: 0183-2508250 Email ID: frroasr@nic.in
Bangalore	Office of the FRRO, MHA, No.55, Double Road, Indiranagar, Bangalore – 560038.Telephone No: 25202052 / 25297683 Email ID: frroblr-ka@nic.in
Hyderabad	Besides Vijaya Bank Counter, Rajiv Gandhi Terminal, Begumpet Old Airport, Hyderabad, Telephone No: 27900211, 27901022, 27900388

Passport Surrender & Renunciation

Passport surrender rules require that Indian nationals, on acquiring foreign citizenship should:

- Notify the nearest Indian consulate.
- Duly renounce their Indian citizenship.
- Pay the appropriate fee.
- Surrender the last Indian passport they held, to the Indian consulate, for cancellation.

While these rules may have been on the books for a long time, they were not strictly enforced until October 2009. The government of India apparently became aware of situations, where former Indian citizens continued to use their Indian passports as travel documents, even after they had acquired foreign citizenship.

In an effort to stop the misuse of Indian passports in such situations, the passport surrender rules were announced. Passport surrender and formal renunciation of Indian citizenship is now compulsory.

For those who acquired foreign citizenship after June 1, 2010. The procedure is simple. They:

- Fill in the appropriate form.
- Submit their last held Indian passport for cancellation.
- Pay the appropriate fee.
- Their passport is then duly cancelled by the Indian consulate officials and they are given a surrender certificate.

DECLARATION OF RENUNCIATION OF CITIZENSHIP OF INDIA ON ACQUISTION OF CITIZENSHIP OF ANOTHER COUNTRY

1. I ______________________________(here insert name and address of declarant) am of full age and capacity and was born at (with Tehsil, District, State and Country __________on ____________(date)

2. I have/have not been married.

3. I acquired US /Foreign Nationality on ____________ (date) and consequently have obtained US /Foreign passport no.: __________ dated ______________________

.

4. I hereby renounce my citizenship of India and surrender my Indian Passport No.________________Date of Issue________________

5. Names and full particulars of my minor children, if any, who are/ were Citizens of India

I,_________________________do solemnly and sincerely declare that the foregoing particulars stated in this declaration are true and I make this solemn declaration conscientiously believing the same to be true. Made and subscribed this __________________day of ______
Name, Phone Number, Email address, US address:

Signature: ____________________________

Documents Required:

1. Indian passport original along with a photocopy of first three and last two pages (if you do not have original passport, then photocopy should be submitted along with the self-affidavit for Lost Indian Passport, If you do not have photocopy of Indian passport also then state the same)
2. US naturalization Certificate copy
3. 3. Photocopy of US passport (first two and last two pages and page containing any amendment)
4. Residence proof (Utility bill/driving license/lease deed)
5. Fees: US$ 175/- for those who acquired citizenship on or after 1 June 2010, others US$ 20/-
6. Mailing fees: US$ 20 (if you are seeking surrender certificate by mail)

Passport Surrender Rules Explained

There are quite a few persons of Indian origin who acquired foreign citizen earlier, before surrender rules were widely announced. Basically, those who acquired foreign citizenship before 31st May 2010, fall into one of the following categories:

- Their passport was cancelled by the Indian consulate and they already have a cancelled stamp on their last Indian passport.
- They acquired foreign citizenship before 31st May 2010 and do not have a cancelled stamp on their last Indian passport.
- They acquired foreign citizenship more than 10 years ago and have lost their Indian passport.

While only the Indian consulate officials can answer specific queries on this topic. Here is what currently appears to be applicable:

1. Those who acquired foreign citizenship on or after 1 June, 2010 are required to obtain a surrender certificate from the Indian consulate that is applicable to their jurisdiction.

2. If the last Indian passport you held, before acquiring foreign citizenship, has been cancelled by an Indian consulate and you acquired foreign citizenship on or before May 31, 2010. You do not need to get a surrender certificate. In such cases you should keep your old Indian passport for reference.

3. If you became a foreign citizen before June 1, 2010 and your last Indian passport has not been cancelled, then you are

required to apply for a surrender certificate. In such cases your passport will be cancelled, and you will be issued a surrender or renunciation certificate. Your passport with the cancelled stamp will be returned to you.

4. In case you became a foreign citizen more than 10 years ago, and have lost the last Indian passport you held, you can obtain a deemed surrender certificate.

♦♦♦

Surrender & Renunciation Certificate Difference

Once you acquire foreign citizenship and renounce your Indian citizenship, the procedure basically involves surrendering your passport for cancellation. Once cancelled the passport is returned to you and a **'Surrender Certificate'** issued.

Those who have misplaced or lost their last Indian passports several years back and hence do not have a passport that they can surrender for cancellation, are given a **'Renunciation Certificate**'. Whether you get a surrender or renunciation certificate they both have the same effect.

♦♦♦

Passport Surrender Penalties

Former Indian citizens, if they fail to surrender their passports in a timely manner, or have used their Indian passports for travel, are charged penalties by the authorities.

While such penalties are subject to revision/change at any time by the government of India, the current information is provided.

- If your last Indian passport expired before January 1, 2005 there are no penalties.
- If your last Indian passport expired after January 1, 2005 and has a cancelled stamp then there are no penalties.
- In case your passport does not have a cancelled stamp, and more than three years have passed, since you acquired foreign citizenship, there is a penalty of US$250.
- In case your Indian passport was used for travel to India three months after you acquired foreign citizenship, then there is a penalty of US$250 for each time it was used. The maximum penalty in such cases is US$ 1250.
  Those who are not in the United States will probably pay the equivalent amount, in their local currency.
- Persons of Indian origin who acquired foreign citizenship more than 10 years ago, and have lost the last Indian passport they held, can obtain a deemed surrender certificate.
  The deemed surrender certificate is considered proof of renunciation of Indian citizenship. The fee is currently US$20. In case services are done by an outsourced company, there may be an additional fee.

Documents required to get surrender certificate

- Renunciation Form duly filled.
- Your most recent Indian passport that you held when you acquired foreign citizenship
- Copy of your currently held foreign passport
- Proof of Address

Renunciation of Indian Citizenship fees

The renunciation fee currently is US$175. However the fee payable depends on when you acquired foreign citizenship.

1. Those who acquire foreign citizenship on or after June 1, 2010 pay fees of $175.00. The total fee currently in USA is US$ 195 after adding service charges of the outsourcing company.
2. Persons who acquired foreign citizenship on or before May 31, 2010 are not being charged the renunciation fee and will pay miscellaneous fee of $25.00. The total fee currently in USA is US$45 after adding service charges of the outsourcing company.

Outsourcing of services by Indian Consulates

In the United States with effect from May 21, 2014 the Visa, OCI, Renunciation of Indian citizenship application collection etc. have been outsourced to Cox & Kings Global Services Pvt. Ltd. Their Website address is http://www.in.ckgs.us

In the United Kingdom the High Commission of India, London and its Consulate General in Birmingham & Edinburgh have outsourced the handling of 'Surrender of Indian Passport Services' to VF Services (UK) Ltd. Their website address is: http://in.vfsglobal.co.uk/

Outsourcing companies may change at the discretion of the Government of India.

♦♦♦

Indian - Visa Options

After acquiring foreign citizenship, former Indian citizens require a visa to visit India. There are several types of visas issued for visiting India, normally a change of purpose for which a visa has been issued is not allowed. By selecting the appropriate visa that will fit your travel plans, you may save yourself time and money in the long run.

Two month gap period rule for tourist visa

Tourist visas are the most common type of visa. In 2009, a new rule was announced by the Indian government regarding tourist visas. Foreign nationals holding tourist visas with multiple entry facility were required to have a gap of at least 2 months between two visits to India.

According to this rule, once a tourist leaves India, they could not return to India until at least two months had lapsed. In case a foreign national wanted to visit India again within the two month period, they were required to obtain special permission from Indian consulates. This restriction has now been lifted, see below.

Two month gap period rule now removed

For citizens of most countries the TWO months gap between two visits has been removed by the Government of India from 4th Dec 2012.

The two month gap rule however, still applies to nationals of China, Iran, Pakistan, Iraq, Sudan, Bangladesh, Afghanistan, foreigners of Pakistan and Bangladesh origin and stateless persons.

Types of Indian Visa

There are several different types of visas available. The type of visa a person should acquire would of course depend, on the purpose of their trip to India. Every Indian visa is issued with the stipulation that the visa must be used only for the purpose it was issued for.

This 'no change of purpose' rule should not be taken lightly. In case authorities discover, even after a person has visited and left India that he/she had conducted activities other than tourism while having a tourist visa, they can be denied visas in future.

Example:
Tourist visa holder cannot decide to start studying in India. This would be illegal. If intention is to study in India, then a student visa is required and this must be taken before arriving in India because change of visa type is not allowed from within India. Similarly, a journalist cannot come to India on a tourist visa in their professional capacity, they need a journalist visa.

The many different types of visas that are issued by the Government of India are described briefly on the next page. Readers are advised to confirm visa information with the Indian consulates as rules and regulations can be changed by the Government of India at their discretion.

The type of visa required to travel to India depends on the reason for which the travel is being undertaken. When applying for an Indian visa, applicants must specify the purpose of their intended visit. Apply for the type of visa that meets the purpose of your visit.

Tourist Visa

Tourist Visa is granted to those who visit India for tourism purposes such as, sightseeing, visiting family and friends etc. No other activity is allowed on a tourist visa.

Tourist visas are normally valid for 6 months to 1 year with single or multiple entries. Irrespective of the duration of validity of visa, on each visit the maximum period of stay in India is limited to 6 months (180 days) only.

Nationals of China, Iran, Pakistan, Iraq, Sudan, Bangladesh, Afghanistan and also foreigners of Pakistan, Bangladesh origin have to abide by the two month gap rule, which requires that there should be a gap of at least 2 months between two separate visits to India.

Fast Electronic Tourist Visa (e-TV)

The electronic visa scheme previously known as 'Visa on Arrival' was launched by The Indian Government of India in January 2010. Since visa application for this type of visa had to be made prior to arrival in India, the visa name was subsequently changed to electronic tourist visa (e-TV) so as to avoid any misunderstanding.

Citizens of 77 countries are currently eligible to avail the e-TV visa facility. List of countries is provided on page 64.

How to apply for electronic Indian tourist visa

Applicants of eligible countries can apply online at least 4 days before their arrival date in India and within a 30 day window. See example for clarification.

Example: Suppose a person applies for electronic visa online on April 1st 2016. Then the earliest arrival date can be after at least 4 days which would be in this case April 5, 2016. The latest arrival date that can be selected within the 30 day allowed window would be May 4, 2016.

Electronic Tourist Visa (e-TV) Eligibility

Electronic tourist visa for India is available to citizens of 77 countries currently. Some of the conditions apply to applicants of this type of visa:

- Purpose of visit to India should be recreation, sightseeing, casual visit to meet friends or relatives, short duration medical treatment or a casual business visit.
- Passport should have at least six months validity from date of arrival and two blank pages for stamping purposes by Indian immigration officers.
- Travelers must have a return ticket
- The validity of this type of visa is for 30 days from the date of arrival. Only single entry visa is issued and is non-extendable. This type of visa can also not be converted to another type of visa after entry.
- Travelers must enter India via designated airports. They are: Ahmedabad, Amritsar, Bengaluru, Chennai, Cochin, Delhi, Gaya, Goa, Hyderabad, Jaipur, Kolkata, Lucknow, Mumbai, Tiruchirapalli, Trivandrum & Varanasi. Travelers when leaving India can **exit** from any of the authorized Immigration 'Check Posts' in India
- The fee currently is US$ 60/- per applicant. Fee should be paid online when submitting visa application.

To apply for an electronic tourist visa online:

1. Visit: https://indianvisaonline.gov.in/visa/tvoa.html
2. Apply online
3. Pay visa fee online
4. Electronic visa confirmation is emailed to applicant
5. Print visa confirmation and take printout when going to India as it will be required at point of entry.

List of countries approved for electronic Indian tourist visa

Andorra	Ecuador	Marshall Islands	Russia
Anguilla	El Salvador	Mauritius	Saint Kitts & Nevis
Antigua & Barbuda	Estonia	Mexico	Saint Lucia
Argentina	Fiji	Micronesia	St Vincent
Armenia	Finland	Monaco	Samoa
Aruba	France	Mongolia	Seychelles
Australia	Georgia	Montenegro	Singapore
Bahamas	Germany	Montserrat	Slovenia
Barbados	Grenada	Mozambique	Solomon Islands
Belgium	Guatemala	Myanmar	Spain
Belize	Guyana	Nauru	Sri Lanka
Bolivia	Haiti	Netherlands	Suriname
Brazil	Honduras	New Zealand	Sweden
Cambodia	Hungary	Nicaragua	
	Indonesia		

Canada Cayman Island Chile China China- SAR Hong Kong China- SAR Macau Colombia Cook Islands Costa Rica Cuba Djibouti Dominica Dominican Republic	Ireland Israel East Timor Jamaica Japan Jordan Kenya Kiribati Laos Latvia Liechtenstein Lithuania Luxembourg Malta Malaysia Oman	Niue Island Norway Palau Palestine Panama Papua New Guinea Paraguay Peru Philippines Poland Portugal Republic of Korea Rep of Macedonia	Taiwan Tanzania Thailand Tonga Turks/Caicos Island Tuvalu UAE Ukraine United Kingdom USA Uruguay Vanuatu Vatican City Venezuela Vietnam.

Business Visa

Those who plan to conduct business in India should apply for a business visa. A 'Business Visa' is granted to those who conduct business in India such as, making sales or establishing contacts on behalf of a company outside India. Business Visa is not for employment purposes.

Business visas may be valid for 6 months to one year or more, with single or multiple entries, depending on your requirements. Irrespective of the duration of validity of visa, on each visit the maximum period of stay in India is limited to 6 months (180 days) only.

Those who are applying to work for an Indian company should apply for an Employment Visa.

Employment Visa

An Employment Visa is granted to those persons who are employees of an Indian company, or preform honorary work (without salary) with registered NGOs in India.

Indian Consulates may grant 'Employment visa' valid for a limited validity irrespective of the duration of the contract. Further extension up to 5 years could be obtained from Ministry of Home Affairs or FRRO in the concerned State in India.

To be considered for 'Employment Visa' all foreign workers must earn the equivalent of $25,000 per annum or more.

Student Visa

Student visa is granted to genuine students, to pursue regular studies at recognized institutions in India. Visa is valid for the period of study as approved by the educational institution in India, for multiple entries.

Entry Visa

An Entry Visa is granted for a specific purpose (short term courses and unpaid internships) or other non-business related purposes. An Invitation letter is required from concerned organization/authorities in India.

Members of the family of a person employed in India are also eligible for Entry visa. In the latter case, documents establishing the employment of the spouse, along with a copy of his/her Employment visa must be attached.

Foreign nationals who own property in India can apply for a one year Entry Visa. This type of visa can be extended later, by the Foreigners Regional Registration Officer in India, on a yearly basis up to a maximum period of 5 years.

Long Term Entry Visa

Long term, 5 years entry visa is normally issued to people of Indian origin only. Five and ten year tourist visas were available preciously only to US citizens under a bilateral arrangement.

Prime Minister Modi during his visit to Canada on April 15, 2015 announced that Canadian citizens would also be eligible for 10 year Indian visas. Now 10-Year multiple-entry Tourist and Business Visa are available to Canadian nationals also.

Persons of Indian origin may however find it more prudent, to simply get an OCI card which is a lifetime visa.

♦♦♦

Conference Visa

A Conference visa is granted for people who wish to attend international conferences in India. Those seeking conference visas should apply in a timely manner. Indian consulates normally issue this type of visa, only after clearance of the conference is received from the Government of India.

Journalist Visa

A Journalist Visa is granted to professional journalists and photographers. Journalist visas generally have a validity of three months with single entry. Those who intend to make a documentary in India are required to contact the Press and Information wing in the Indian Embassy.

Research Visa

A Research Visas is granted to 'Research Professors or Scholars' who wish to conduct research work in India. Applicants need to obtain prior permission from the concerned authorities to conduct research projects in India. Validity of a Research visa usually coincides with the research period.

Transit Visa

A transit visa is granted to enable the holder to travel through India to reach their ultimate destination. Change of purpose is not allowed. Transit visa is valid for direct transit only within 15 days of date of issue, for a maximum period of 3 days with single or double entry.

♦♦♦

Medical Visa

A Medical visa is granted to those who need to travel to India for medical treatment. Visa is valid for up to three months with single entry. Documents explaining details of the treatment from the concerned hospitals/doctors are normally required.

Medical Escort Visa

A Medical Escort visa is granted to a person who has to accompany a patient travelling to India for medical treatment. This type of visa is normally given to a close relative/family member or a friend of the patient. This type of visa is valid for up to three months for a single entry.

The patient in such cases would need a medical visa, and the escort would apply for a medical escort visa.

Transferring valid visa to new passport

Those who have a long term visa and their passports are expiring, can get their visa transferred to their new passport. In case you need to travel and there is not enough time, then the option is to simply take your expired passport that has a valid visa stamped on it, along with the new passport when travelling.

How to transfer Visa to new passport

- Applicants need to submit their old passport that has the valid Indian visa stamped on it.
- Submit their new passport on which the visa is to be transferred.
- Submit the required fee for this service.
- Visa can only be transferred from the respective Indian consulate where it was originally issued.
- To transfer a visa, there should be a remaining validity of at least one month (30 days) on the day you submit your application.

No Requirement to Transfer OCI Visa

The requirement to carry your old passport showing the OCI 'U' visa has been withdrawn by the government of India.

As of January 29, 2015 the requirement to carry the old passport with U visa stamp along with new passport has been removed. Now OCI holders can simply carry their OCI booklet as proof of their OCI status along with their foreign passport.

Restricted Areas

Some places in India are designated as Restricted or Protected Areas by the Government of India. Foreigners are not allowed to visit these restricted and protected areas unless they have a permit allowing them to do so, from the concerned authorities.

A tourist visa is not sufficient to visit areas that are designated a 'Restricted/Protected Area, even OCI holders cannot visit such area's without a permit.

List of Restricted Areas

The Protected Areas are as follows:

- Parts of State of Manipur
- Parts of State of Mizoram
- Parts of State of Arunachal Pradesh
- Whole of State of Nagaland
- Whole of State of Sikkim
- Parts of State of Uttaranchal.
- Parts of State of Jammu and Kashmir
- Parts of State of Rajasthan.
- Parts of State of Himachal Pradesh.

The Restricted Areas are as follows:

- Entire Union Territory of Andaman and Nicobar Islands
- Part of the state of Sikkim

There is also a condition that foreign tourists seeking permits to visit these areas, must be accompanied by a recognized travel agent acting as their escort during their visit.

Some tour operators in India also provide help to get these permits on your behalf. Generally its part of the tour package they sell to visit restricted/protected areas. Currently the fee for a permit to visit restricted or protected areas is Indian Rupees 1395/-

Permits to travel to restricted areas are issued only to groups of tourists consisting of two or more people.

In case only one person wishes to get a permit they would have to apply to the Ministry of Home Affairs for approval.

Citizens of Afghanistan, China, Pakistan and foreign nationals of Pakistani origin are also required to get prior approval from the Ministry of Home Affairs to get permits for restricted or protected areas.

Tax Clearance Certificate Requirement to Leave India

The requirement of a tax clearance certificate to leave India was abolished effective January 1, 2003 for most people.

Under current rules, most people when leaving India by land, sea or air are not required to furnish a tax clearance certificate to the airlines, etc. when leaving India.

The only exception here is, when the income tax authorities in India specifically notify the immigration/customs authorities not to allow specific persons to leave India without obtaining a Tax Clearance Certificate. The likelihood is that these persons would also have been advised by the authorities that they would require tax clearance certificate before being allowed to leave India.

What is a tax clearance certificate?

This is a document that certifies that the person to whom the tax clearance certificate is issued:

- Does not owe any taxes to the Indian tax authorities or
- They have made satisfactory arrangements, for payment of any existing tax liabilities that may become payable by them.

Satisfactory arrangement for payment of taxes could be in the form of an employer guarantee, or any other person that is acceptable to the income tax authorities. Such tax clearance certificate is usually given in FORM NO.33.

Persons who may require tax clearance on departure

- Persons, who the tax department believes, are likely to leave India for good, and against whom there is a present or anticipated tax liability. In such cases the officers at departure points are notified. A copy of the information is also sent to the person concerned for their information.
- People who are not domiciled in India and are in India for employment purposes.
- Persons domiciled in India, leaving India as emigrants.

Persons who may not require tax clearance certificate

- Persons below the age of eighteen years.
- Persons, who are not domiciled in India, provided that the person's continuous stay in India at a time does not exceed 120 days.
- Persons who are for the time being, holding any civil post, under the Union or a State or a local authority, and all persons who are for the time being holding posts connected with defense. Their wives are also exempt from this requirement.
- Diplomatic Envoys accredited to India and their wives. Officials of the UN and its specialized Agencies to whom the United Nations (Privilege and Immunities) Act, 1947 applies and their wives.
- Officials of foreign governments functioning in India,

who are exempt from payment of Income tax in India, under agreement between India and the foreign government and the wives of such officials.

- Persons permitted by the Protector of Emigrants to depart out of India to Sri Lanka, Burma or Malaya for unskilled work.
- Persons permitted by the Protector of Emigrants under the Indian Emigration Act 1922, to be recruited for skilled work in an overseas country, except those in respect of whom the Protector at Emigrants declares that a Tax Clearance or an Exemption certificate is necessary.
- Seamen holding Indian Continuous Discharge Certificates, proceeding from India under an agreement of service with a ship owner or an Agent or a Master of a ship, provided that the employers agree to be responsible for the payment of tax due from the seamen in respect of their wages.
- Seamen holding Foreign Continuous Discharge Certificates proceeding from India under an agreement of service with a ship owner or an Agent or Master of a ship, provided that their preceding stay in India was of a duration not exceeding 90 days.
- Persons proceeding on pilgrimage by sea to Iran and Iraq, provided that they travel in deck class with return tickets, hold pilgrim passes, and are not in possession of international passports.

♦♦♦

How to get a Tax Clearance Certificate

Application to get Income tax clearance certificates are made to the income tax department assessing officers, on Form 31 (Application for a Certificate under Section 230(1) of the Income Tax Act, 1961). If no taxes are outstanding or where satisfactory arrangement for payment of taxes due have been made, the Assessing Officer may issue an authorization on Form 32 (Authorization from assessing Income-tax Officer)

The authorization on Form 32 will enable the applicant, to get a proper Tax Clearance Certificate from the concerned tax authority.

♦♦♦

Sample of tax clearance form

Form No. 33 *(See rule 43)*
Clearance Certificate u/s. 230(1)
Clearance Certificate under section 230(1) of the Income-tax Act, 1961

Folio No.______

Government of India

1. Full name (in block letters)__________________
2. Name of father (or husband)_________________
3. Passport No./Emergency Certificate No._______

This is to certify that above mentioned applicant has

* (a) no liabilities outstanding

* (b) made satisfactory arrangements for the payment of taxes which are or may become payable under the Income-tax Act, 1961 (43 of 1961), the Indian Income-tax Act, 1922 (11 of 1922), the Excess Profits Tax Act, 1940 (15 of 1940), the Business Profits Tax Act, 1947 (21 of 1947), the Wealth-tax Act, 1957 (27 of 1957), the Expenditure Tax Act, 1957 (29 of 1957), or the Gift tax Act, 1958 (18 of 1958).

This certificate is valid for a journey or journeys to be commenced on or after and before
Place:
Date:

Assessing Officer Foreign Section

(SEAL) *Strike out the paragraph which is not applicable

Pan Card

PAN refers to a ten-digit alphanumeric number, issued by the Income Tax Department of India in the form of a laminated card; hence we refer to them as **'Pan Cards'**. A Permanent Account Number (PAN) helps identify you, for tax purposes in India.

Myths about Pan Number

There may be some non-residents, who feel that the PAN is some sort of a scheme by the Indian government to keep an eye on their citizens. This is just a myth. PAN is just an identification number, similar to a **'Social Security Number'** in the United States **or 'Social Insurance Number'** in Canada.

What do the numbers on your PAN mean

While the numbers on PAN cards are generated to create a unique number, there are some characteristics associated with the PAN numbers that a person can identify, by simply looking at the card. The fourth character of a PAN will be either the alphabet **P, F, C, H, A** or **T. Where:**

- '**P**' stands for Individual
- '**F**' stands for Firm;
- '**C**' stands for Company,
- '**H**' stands for HUF (Hindu Undivided Family)
- '**A**' stands for AOP (Association of Persons)
- '**T**' stands for Trust etc.

The fifth character of PAN represents first character of the PAN holder's last name/surname.

PAN – Excellent form of photo ID

While the social security/number cards in USA & Canada do not have photographs. The Indian PAN number is much more advanced and in fact, an excellent form of photo ID that is widely accepted across India.

Not All PAN Card holders have to file tax returns

Despite what some may think, it is not mandatory for everyone who has a PAN to file income tax returns every year in India. Tax returns are required only if you have taxable income in India. On the other hand NOT having a PAN does not exempt anyone from avoiding taxes.

Many foreign nationals of Indian origin, who earn interest on their bank accounts in India, already pay income tax in India. Banks deduct tax at source (TDS) on bank accounts and submit the taxes to the tax department. The fact that an account holder does not have a PAN, results in the maximum rate of TDS being deducted.

Pan Card Requirement for Non Residents

While it is understandable that Pan Cards are required by Indian citizens, the question often asked is, whether persons of Indian origin, who have now acquired foreign citizenship need a Pan Card.

Effective 1st January 2007, all Non-Resident Indians and Persons of Indian Origin, need a PAN card to invest in the Indian stock markets. (Foreign investors would also need a PAN).

PAN not compulsory for PIO/OCI holders

Persons of Indian Origin or OCI holders settled abroad, generally have no obligation to get a PAN, unless they have taxable income to declare in India or invest in the Indian stock market.

Should Persons of Indian origin get a PAN

While a PAN card may not be mandatory, for persons of Indian origin residing abroad, there are some benefits of having a PAN. Especially for those NRIs who continue to have close ties with India, have bank accounts in India or own property in India.

Benefits of having PAN Card

- Pan card is an excellent form of acceptable Identity document throughout India. Pan cards have the holder's photo but not their address; hence PAN cards cannot be used as proof of address.
- In the absence of a PAN, banks in India actually deduct the maximum tax as TDS, from the interest earned on bank accounts.
- If you have a NRO account in India, then tax is automatically deducted by your bank on the interest you receive. Some or perhaps all the money deducted (TDS) may be claimed as a refund depending on your income. However, to get a refund, you must file a tax return, which cannot be done unless you have a PAN.
- Thinking of buying a vehicle in India? You will need a Pan for registration of the vehicle. Also many other types of services in India may also require a PAN.

- Investment accounts in India, such as a Demat account, cannot be opened unless you have a PAN.

Therefore there are benefits to having a PAN card. Even if you presently don't require it, your circumstances can quickly change and since a PAN number is valid for life it's better to be prepared.

Keep in mind that just because you have a PAN, it does not mean that you have to file taxes in India, unless you have taxable income to declare in India.

There are no difficult procedures involved in getting a PAN card these days. Non-residents settled abroad now have the facility to request a PAN online by visiting the appropriate website and filling the required form. The procedure on how to get a PAN card is shown below.

♦♦♦

How to get a new Pan Card

Non-residents who wish to apply for a PAN online can visit https://tin.tin.nsdl.com/pan/ and from the menu displayed select 'New PAN for Foreign Citizens (Form 49AA) option. Applications for a new PAN card can be made either from within India or from abroad.

Applying for Pan Card from Abroad

Applications for PAN can be made from many countries online. To start off, Login to the Indian government income tax departments website: https://tin.tin.nsdl.com/pan/index.html

Their website is very well laid out and user friendly. Select the appropriate form depending on your citizenship.

- ✓ Form 49A applies to Indian Citizens
- ✓ Form 49AA applies to Foreign Citizens

After selecting the appropriate Form, follow the simple instructions that are provided to fill the form.

How to check if your PAN is valid

Those who got a PAN several years earlier, or perhaps got their PAN through agents by paying a fee, may sometimes wonder whether their PAN card is valid or not.

The Indian Income tax department provides a facility where a person can check the status of their PAN on the internet.

How to check your PAN card status online

The method of checking PAN information online is quite simple

- Log on to: https://incometaxindiaefiling.gov.in/e-Filing/Services/KnowYourPanLink.html
- Fill in your first name, middle name, surname and date of birth.
- Confirm that information that you entered is correct, use the exact date format as shown in form. Click the submit button. Your PAN details such as number, name and jurisdiction will be shown on the screen.

NRIs exempt from quoting PAN

The government has made quoting of PAN compulsory in India for specified transactions. Non-residents however, are exempt from these provisions. Those who are exempt can normally use 'Form 60' in lieu of providing PAN.

NRIs who find themselves in a situation where they are asked to produce a PAN card to avail a service or make a purchase in India. Should request for and fill out Form 60 which should be accepted in lieu of PAN. When filling form 60, you will also have to provide proof of your address.

A sample of Form 60 is available on our website. To view visit http://nriinformation.com/faq1/index_htm_files/form60.pdf

Documents as proof of address when using Form 60

As proof of address when using 'Form 60' in lieu of PAN, any of the following documents can be used as proof of address:

- Ration Card
- Passport
- Driving license
- Identity Card issued by any institution
- Copy of the electricity bill or telephone bill showing residential address
- Any document or communication issued by any authority or Central Government, State Government or local bodies showing residential address
- Any other documentary evidence in support of address given on the declaration.

Documents accepted as proof of identity

For proof of identity the following documents are normally accepted:

- Passport
- Driving License
- Aadhaar Card.
- Government issued photo ID

Generally many foreign passports do not mention the address of the passport holder. Hence for such persons the use of their passport as proof of address is not possible. Even if address is not shown on your passport it can still be used as proof of identity.

PAN Card Fee

PAN Card fee currently is Indian Rupees 106/- for applicants applying in India, who have an Indian address for the PAN card to be sent to. Applicants who apply from abroad are required to pay Rupees 985/- due to the cost of sending documents abroad.

Some agents in India advertise to actually collect documents etc. from your home, and do the filling on your behalf for a fee. Advertisements in some websites also offer such services to non-residents. Generally such schemes ask NRIs to mail their documents to these people in India, they promise to apply on their behalf for PAN cards and send it to them in a few days. Be very careful before sending your identity documents to someone unknown to you.

Non-residents are especially prone to such agents as NRIs are not present in the country. Identity theft is a major problem so do take care and act accordingly to safeguard your identity.

Paying PAN Card Fee from Abroad

The fee for processing PAN application from abroad is Rupees 985 which includes the application fee of Rupees. 93 + dispatch charges of Rupees 771 and a 14% service tax.

While paying the extra mailing charges to have their PAN cards sent abroad probably is not a problem for many non-residents, the mode for sending the payment does cause difficulty for many NRIs. Even though payments can be made by credit cards, NRIs often have difficulty paying with foreign issued credit cards.

Those who apply for PAN from abroad are left with no alternatives but to send a demand draft as payment. Getting a draft in Rupees is not easy for many NRIs, unless there is a State Bank of India branch or other bank that has links to India located near their area of residence.

AO Number on Pan Card Application

Some non-residents may be confused as to which AO number to select when applying for Pan Card. Those who are unaware of their AO Code can select the default AO Code (DLC-C-35-1) as their AO Code.

♦♦♦

How to make changes to your PAN card record

Most services connected to PAN are done online. Some web addresses to access services related to PAN are provided on the next page.

- To correct information on PAN that you already have, go to: https://tin.tin.nsdl.com/pan/changerequest.html
- For PAN card grievances, such as having not received your PAN: http://incometax.sparshindia.com/pan/PAN.asp?id=1
- Owning or using more than one PAN is against law. To rectify such a situation you can cancel your duplicate PAN go to: http://incometax.sparshindia.com/pan/newPAN.asp
- You can know status of your grievance relating to your application for PAN by visiting: http://incometax.sparshindia.com/pan/PAN.asp?id=2
- For more information on PAN you can visit the Income tax department of India website, their website address is: http://www.incometaxindia.gov.in/

♦♦♦

Pan card requirement to make cash purchase

When paying for goods or services in cash where the amount is over Rupees 50,000, there is a requirement in India that PAN card should be provided. To identify the person paying in cash.

NRIs, OCI holders and PIO in the event they do not have a PAN Card can fill in Form No 60 which should be acceptable. It is not mandatory for non-residents to have PAN and filling this form allows such people to pay in cash without producing a PAN Card. The place you are conducting business at and paying in cash will normally have copies of form 60 available and request that you fill it out so that they will be in compliance of the law.

Sample of form to use if you don't have PAN

Form No. 60 of Income tax Rules, 1962

Form of Declaration to be filed by a person who does not have either a Permanent Account Number or General Index Register Number and who makes payment in cash in respect of transactions specified in clauses (a) to (h) of rule 114B

1. Full name and address of the declarant: ....
2. Particulars of transaction:
3. Amount of the transaction:
4. Are you assessed to tax? Yes/No
5. If yes,

(i) Details of Ward/Circle/Range where the last return of Income was filed?
(ii) Reasons for not having Permanent Account Number/ General Index Register Number6. Details of the document being produced in support of address in Column (1)
....

Verification

I, ... do hereby declare that what is stated above is true to the best of my knowledge and belief.

Verified today, the .... day of ....20.....

Date: ....

Place: ....

Signature of the declarant

Taxation in India

Taxation in India and Dual taxation are topics that are of concern to most non-resident Indians across the globe. Several questions that I receive from visitors of my NRI Information website are related to taxation in India.

The most common questions are:

- Will I be taxed in India if I visit India and stay there for more than 60 days in a year?
- Will I have to file income tax return in India if I spend six months in India?
- Will I have to pay tax on my foreign income in India if I spend more than 182 days in India?

Let's consider the three questions mentioned above:

1. Simply visiting India for 60 days does not make a tourist liable to file tax returns in India.
2. A tax return is required to be filed in India if a person has taxable income. The mere fact, that a person spends more than 182 days in India does not make them liable to file an income tax return.
3. By staying in India for 182 days in a financial year, you become a resident for tax purposes in India. That is any income you earn in India, is taxable in India. However, simply staying in India over 182 days does not automatically make your foreign income taxable in India. NRIs depending on the length of stay abroad before returning to India may qualify for Resident but Not Ordinarily Resident (RNOR)

status which exempts their foreign income from being taxed in India. More information on RNOR (also referred to as NOR) is provided on page 93 of this book.

NRI global income not taxed by simply staying more than 182 days in India

NRIs should not assume that just because they stay in India more than 182 days, their worldwide income will become taxable in India.

Although a stay over 182 days makes you a resident and any income sourced in India becomes taxable, your foreign income is exempt from Indian taxes if you have been non-resident in India for 9 out of 10 immediately preceding financial years, or if your stay in India does not total 730 days or more, in the preceding 7 financial years.

When should NRIs file income tax returns in India?

If you are an NRI, you would have to file Indian income tax return for a financial year if you satisfy either of two conditions mentioned below:

- You have earned short-term or long-term capital gains, from sale of any investments or assets, even if the gains are less than the basic exemption limit.

  Or

- Your taxable income in India during financial year in question was above the basic exemption limit.

The basic exemption for the financial year 2015-2016 is Rupees 2.5 lakh. In case you are a senior citizen, your exemption is still Rs.2.5 and not Rs. 3 lakh that senior residents in India are allowed. NRIs should note that the enhanced exemption limit for senior citizens is applicable only to residents and not to non-residents.

Suppose your only income in India that was derived from:

- Your bank accounts, such as interest income.
- Capital gains income.

If tax by way of TDS was deducted at source from such income, then you need not file a tax return in India, unless you wish to claim a tax refund for some or all the tax deducted at source. Suppose your taxable income for the year was below the allowed basic tax exemption slab. To get a refund of tax deducted as TDS, you can file a tax return.

NRI taxation in India

Whether an NRI is liable to pay taxes in India, depends on their residency status and the source of income. Persons of Indian Origin who return to India for permanent settlement, should be aware that at some point of time, their foreign income may also become taxable in India.

In India, citizenship is not the only factor used to decide a person's tax liability. Residential status in India is important for accessing tax liability of a person. However, some types of income, such as rental income may attract tax, regardless of your residential status in India.

The Income tax Act, 1961, is the governing authority for

taxation in India. There are three types of residential status classifications that are considered for tax purposes.

♦♦♦

Types of residential status categories for tax purposes

1. Resident and Ordinarily Resident (ROR).
2. Non Resident (NR)
3. Resident and Ordinarily Resident (RNOR) also known as NOR.

Regardless of which countries citizenship a person holds, they would fall into one of the three categories of residency.

Conditions that make NRIs resident for tax purposes

You can be deemed to be a resident of India for taxation purposes if during a financial year, which is from 1st April to 31st March, any one of the following conditions is satisfied:

1. You are present in India for 182 days or more in the year; or
2. You are present in India for 60 days or more
   and
   within the four previous years, you have been in India for a total of 365 days or more.

Note: The stay in India need not be continuous.

If you satisfy any of the above conditions, you are considered a resident in India (ROR) for tax purposes.

Tax liability of 'Resident and Ordinarily Resident'

Those who fall under the 'Resident and Ordinarily Resident category' (**ROR)**, are required to pay tax in India on their worldwide income, wherever accrued or received.

NRIs however, can avoid paying taxes on their global income if they qualify for 'Resident but **Not** Ordinarily Resident' status.

To qualify for 'Resident but Not Ordinarily Resident' (RNOR) for a tax year, either of the following conditions must be satisfied:

- You have been non-resident in India for 9 of the previous 10 years; **or**
- Your presence in India during the previous 7 years has been less than 730 days.

If **any one** of the above conditions is satisfied, you are 'Not Ordinarily Resident' in India. In this case you only pay tax on your Indian income and your foreign income is exempt from tax in India.

On the other hand if you **none** of the above conditions are satisfied, then you are considered an ordinary resident for taxation purposes.

Residents for tax purposes in India (ROR) are subject to tax on their worldwide income. Their Indian income as well as their foreign income becomes taxable in India. However, tax agreements (DTAA) may provide some relief from taxation of foreign income in India.

♦♦♦

Tax liability of 'Resident but Not Ordinarily Resident'

An **RNOR** is required to pay tax on taxable Indian income. Foreign income is exempt from Indian taxes, unless the foreign income is derived from a business controlled in, or by a profession set up in India. RNOR status category is designed to help non-residents, who return to India for settlement after a long period of time.

NRIs when they relocate to India for permanent settlement, will continue to benefit from the exemption of tax on their foreign income as long as they have RNOR status.

RNOR status normally lasts two years, however, by adjusting the dates of their return to India, some non-residents may be able to avail the benefit of RNOR status for three financial years.

A person will be an RNOR if they have been out of India for 9 of last 10 years, or if they have spent less than 729 days in India, in the last 7 years. Only one of the two conditions needs to be satisfied.

Those who have not visited India for 9 years and return to India at the start of a new financial year, may be able to qualify for NOR status for three financial years. The financial year in India is from April 1st to March 31st.

As long as a returning non-resident has NOR status, their foreign earnings remain exempt from Indian taxes. When RNOR status expires they would become liable to pay tax on their foreign income in India. Double Taxation Avoidance Agreements should in most cases, protect them to some extent from paying taxes in

India, on their foreign income.

Example: Mr. Gupta, a person of Indian origin, returns to India from UK after an absence of 9.5 years. He will be deemed to have RNOR status for two years. Any income he earns in UK while living in India for the next two years will not be taxable in India. After two years, Mr. Gupta will be liable to pay tax on his UK income in India. He will however get credit under the double taxation treaty between India and UK and this may help reduce or even eliminate the tax liability in India on his UK income.

Scope of Taxation Based on Residence			
Description	**ROR**	**RNOR**	**Non-Resident**
Income received or deemed to be received in India	Taxable	Taxable	Taxable
Income accruing or arising or deemed to accrue or arise in India	Taxable	Taxable	Taxable
Income deemed to accrue or arise outside India from a business controlled or profession setup in India	Taxable	Taxable	Not Taxable
Other income accruing or arising outside India	Taxable	Not Taxable	Not Taxable

Dual Taxation - DTAA

One of the major concerns that NRIs have is dual taxation. No one wants to pay taxes in two countries and many countries tax their residents on their worldwide income.

To provide some relief from dual taxation to their citizens, many nations have signed bilateral double taxation agreements with each other. These agreements are known as 'Double Tax Avoidance Agreements (DTAA).

The objective of Double Taxation Avoidance Agreements between two countries is to provide some tax relief to their citizens and to avoid taxation of the same income by both countries.

There are generally two ways that DTAA can help.

1. The resident country may exempt income earned in the foreign country ***Or***
2. Grant credits for the tax paid in the other country.

When credit is granted in one country for tax paid on the same income in the other country under DTAA, the tax payer pays no more than the higher of the two tax rates.

Example:

Naveen, an OCI holder in Canada, moves back to India after several years. At some point of time he becomes a resident in India for taxation purposes (ROR) and as per rules, his worldwide income becomes taxable in India. Let's assume he has investments in Canada that earn him $20,000 a year.

1. Naveen would be liable to pay tax in Canada on his

$20,000 income, as the income is generated in Canada.

2. He would also be liable to pay tax on the $20,000 to the Indian tax authorities, as his worldwide income would be taxable in India.

This would mean that Naveen would be paying tax on the same income twice! Fortunately this is where the DTAA helps.

Canada and India have signed the DTAA. Let's assume Naveen pays tax in Canada @20% which works out to $4000. He pays this tax to the Canadian tax authorities. When filing his tax in India, he has to declare his Canadian income as his worldwide income is taxable in India. Under the DTAA Naveen will get credit for the taxes he has already paid in Canada.

If the tax rate is lower or equal in India, he will not have to pay any additional tax in India on his Canadian income. On the other hand if the tax rate is slightly higher in India, he would simply pay the difference.

Double Taxation Avoidance Agreements

India has 'Double Taxation Avoidance Agreements' with several countries. Even in cases where no DTAA exists, India is said to provide tax relief from dual taxation to its residents, to some extent.

DTAA agreements and other agreements for sharing tax information between governments is an ongoing affair. A list of the countries with which India has already signed DTAA agreements is provided on the next page. To read DTAA agreements that India has signed with various countries visit the Indian income-tax website: http://www.incometaxindia.gov.in

Countries that have signed a DTAA Agreement with India		
Armenia	Mongolia	Myanmar
Australia	Montenegro	Namibia
Austria	Morocco	Nepal
Bangladesh	Mozambique	Netherlands
Belarus	Germany	New Zealand
Belgium	Greece	Norway
Botswana	H. Kingdom of Jordan	Oman
Brazil	Hungary	Philippines
Bulgaria	Iceland	Poland
Canada	Indonesia	Portuguese Republic
China	Ireland	Qatar
Cyprus	Kuwait	Confederation
Czech Republic	Kyrgyz Republic	Syrian Arab Republic
Denmark	Libya	Tajikistan
Egypt	Luxembourg	Tanzania
Finland	Malaysia	Thailand
France	Malta	Trinidad and Tobago
Germany	Mauritius	Turkey
Greece	Romania	Turkmenistan
Hungary	Russia	UAE

Iceland	Serbia	UAR (Egypt)
Indonesia	Singapore	UGANDA
Ireland	Slovenia	UK
Israel	South Africa	Ukraine
Italy	Spain	United Mexican St
Japan	Sri Lanka	USA
Kazakhstan	Sudan	Uzbekistan
Kenya	Sweden	Vietnam
Korea	Swiss	Zambia
Saudi Arabia		

Under the Income Tax Act 1961 of India, Section 90, relief is provided for taxpayers who have paid tax to a country with which India has signed a double tax avoidance agreement. India also offers relief to those who have paid tax to countries that do not have a double taxation avoidance agreement with India under Section 91 of the Income Tax Act 1961.

Points to consider on tax treaties (DTAA)

- Even though individuals are considered resident under tax treaty, based on their primary place of residence, this is not the only criteria.
- The United States includes citizens and green card holders wherever living, as subject to taxation in the United States and therefore considered as residents for tax treaty purposes.

- There can be a possibility where an individual may have a primary residence in two countries. Tax agreements take this point into consideration and each treaty will have provisions for such situations.

To give you an example, Canada and India tax treaty address this issue as:

(Excerpt from Canada/India DTAA)

1. For the purposes of this Agreement, the term "resident of a Contracting State" means any person who, under the laws of that State, is liable to tax therein by reason of his domicile, residence, place of management or any other criterion of a similar nature.

2. Where by reason of the provisions of paragraph 1 an individual is a resident of both Contracting States, then his status shall be determined in accordance with the following rules:

(a) he shall be deemed to be a resident of the State in which he has a permanent home available to him; if he has a permanent home available to him in both States,

he shall be deemed to be a resident of the State with which his personal and economic relations are closer (hereinafter referred to as his centre of vital interests);

(b) if the State in which he has his centre of vital interests cannot be determined, or if he has not a permanent home available to him in either State, he shall be deemed to be a resident of the State in which he has an habitual abode;

(c) if he has an habitual abode in both States or in neither of

them, he shall be deemed to be a resident of the State of which he is a national;

(d) if he is a national of both States or of neither of them, the competent authorities of the Contracting States shall settle the question by mutual agreement.

DTAA Summary:

- India provides protection against double taxation, either by complete avoidance of overlapping tax or waiving a certain amount of the tax payable in India.
- India currently has double taxation avoidance treaties signed with most countries in the world. These treaties are periodically reviewed and strengthened in view of the global concern of money laundering activities.

Foreign nationals of several countries such as USA, Canada and UK are required to declare and pay taxes on their worldwide income. Double taxation avoidance treaties, actually help in either minimizing the tax payable to your home country or in some cases even eliminating further tax liabilities, depending on the tax rates applicable.

How to claim tax benefits in India under DTAA

As per amendment to the Indian Income Tax Act announced in the Union Budget 2012. Effective April 1st 2012 to avail benefits under DTAA, NRIs must provide a Tax Residency Certificate (TRC) from the government of the country they reside in.

For example, NRIs living in USA having NRO bank account in India, can avail lower rate of tax deduction (TDS) if they can get a tax residency certificate in USA and provide it to their bank.

Tax Residency Certificate should include the following information:

- Name of the assessee
- Status (individual, company, firm etc.) of the assessee
- Nationality (in case of individual)
- Country or specified territory of incorporation or registration (in case of others)
- Assessee tax identification number in the country or specified territory of residence or in case no such number, then a unique number on the basis of which the person is identified by the Government of the country or the specified territory *(Example social security number etc.)*
- Residential status for the purposes of tax
- Period for which the certificate is applicable
- Address of the applicant for the period for which the certificate is applicable

Information on how to get a tax residency certificate is provided on the next page.

♦♦♦

How to get a tax residency certificate

Tax Residency Certificates are normally issued by the tax authorities of the country of which you are a citizen. For example, U.S. nationals would have to contact the IRS to get such a certificate and UK citizens would approach the HMRC.

Tax residency certificate is a document that basically certifies that a person is a citizen of a country for tax purposes. This certificate entitles individuals to take advantage of benefits that may be available to them under tax treaties between governments.

To get a residency certificate in the United States, an application is made on Form 8802. The tax residency certificate is issued by the IRS as Form 6166. This is a letter printed on U.S. Department of Treasury stationery, certifying that the person named in the document is a resident of the United States, for purposes of the income tax laws of the United States. Currently, the fee for acquiring this certificate in the United States is US$ 85.

- **Canadian citizens** can get a residency certificate from the Canada Revenue Agency (CRA) by applying to the tax office where they normally file their tax returns.
- **UK citizens** can get a certificate of UK residence from the HMRC office which normally deals with their tax affairs. This would be where they normally send their tax returns.
- **Australian citizens**, who require a certificate of residency, can simply send a signed letter or fax to the Australian Tax Office (ATO). There is a fee charged for this service.

Requests for certificate in Australia can be mailed to:
Attn: Certificate of residency/status
Australian Taxation Office
CAS Income Tax and Activity Statement
GPO Box 4991, SYDNEY NSW 2001
Fax to (02) 9374 8999 or (02) 9374 2811.

NRI can save TDS by availing DTAA benefit

Several NRIs have NRO bank accounts in India. The interest earned on account balances held in Indian bank accounts by NRIs, is taxable in India, as this income originates in India. Generally all banks in India currently withhold 30.9% as a tax deduction at source (TDS) from interest income.

Suppose the account holder is a US resident. The DTAA between USA and India under Article 11 Interest states:

1. Interest arising in a Contracting State and paid to a resident of the other Contracting State may be taxed in that other State.
2. However, such interest may also be taxed in the Contracting State in which it arises, and according to the laws of that State, but if the beneficial owner of the interest is a resident of the other Contracting State, the tax so charged shall not exceed:

   (a) 10 percent of the gross amount of the interest if such interest is paid on a loan granted by a bank carrying on a bona fide banking business or by a similar financial institution (including an insurance company); and

(b) 15 percent of the gross amount of the interest in all other cases

USA residents by availing the benefits of the DTAA, can save tax on their Indian bank account interest income by paying 15% tax instead of the 30.9% banks are currently deducting. However to claim this benefit NRIs must provide their banks the following documents:

- Tax Residency Certificate
- Copy of PAN Card
- Self-declaration cum indemnity form (Bank should provide this form or download from their website)
- Copy of Passport and Visa
- Person of Indian origin (PIO) proof

Considering that banks require these documents for every financial year you claim benefits under DTAA and the time and money involved getting and submitting documents, many NRIs I assume simply don't bother.

NRIs who don't bother to get residency certificates and pay the higher TDS automatically deducted by banks, can still get money back if their income in India is below the tax free income allowed. However, to claim refunds, a tax return must be filed in India.

♦♦♦

Paying Taxes in India

Every person, whose total income for the previous year is more than the tax free income allowed for their category is required to file income tax returns in India, under the provisions of the Income-tax Act, 1961.

Tax free income allowed for each category is called a 'slab' in India. The Income 'Tax Slabs' show the amount of income that is exempt from taxes for an individual, in a particular financial year.

Tax Slabs for the Financial Year 2015/2016

Tax slabs are different for Individuals based on age and sex. Currently in India, there are tax slabs set for:

- Individuals up to age 60
- Senior citizens (Those over age 60)
- Super Citizens! (Those over age 80 and over)

NRIs Note: The enhanced exemption limit for senior citizens is applicable only to residents and not to non-residents.

Financial year in India

The financial year in India, is not January to December as in some western countries. In India the financial year for taxation purposes, begins on 1st of April every year and ends on 31st March of the subsequent year.

The financial year in which the income is earned is known as the previous year. The financial year, following a previous year is known as the assessment year.

The assessment year is the year, in which the income earned in the previous year is taxable.

Tax slabs for the financial year 2015-2016

[Tax slabs for seniors not applicable to Non Residents]

Individuals up to Age 60 Income Rupees Tax Slabs 2015 - 2016	Tax Liability
Up to Rs.2,50,000 Between Rs.2,50,001 - Rs.5,00,000 Between Rs.5,00,001 - Rs.10,00,000 Above Rs.10,00,000	Nil 10% 20% 30%
Individuals between age 60 to 80 years	
Up to Rs.3,00,000 Between Rs.3,00,001 - Rs.5,00,000 Between Rs.5,00,001 – Rs10,00,000 Above Rs.10,00,000	Nil 10% 20% 30%
Individuals Age 80 years and over	
Up to Rs.5,00,000 Between Rs.5,00,001 – Rs10,00,000 Above Rs.10,00,000	Nil 20% 30%

Tax Deduction at Source (TDS)

Any non-resident who continues to earn income in India, while living abroad is subject to tax in India. Normally in many instances, such as interest received on NRO bank accounts or perhaps even rental income, tax is deducted in the form of TDS.

Interest earned on NRE accounts, as well as other foreign currency accounts such as FCNR accounts, is tax free in India.

Indian residents, who earn interest on their Indian bank accounts, are liable to pay TDS on amounts over and above Rupees 10,000. However when it comes to NRIs, they are not allowed this benefit on their NRO accounts. All interest earned in NRO accounts, is subject to a TDS rate of a whopping 30.9%.

Interest earned by NRIs on other types of deposits, such as bonds, are subject to a TDS @ 20%. However dividends from equity shares, equity mutual funds and debt mutual funds are exempt in the hands of the share or unit holder.

TDS reduction for PIO under DTAA

NRIs can pay a lower rate of TDS if they are from a country that has a DTAA with India. Citizens of countries such as USA, Canada, UK, and Australia can get away by paying a TDS on interest income of only 15% by virtue of tax treaties between countries.

However, to claim this benefit, the Indian authorities require the individual to submit a 'Tax Residency Certificate'.

As for capital gains, profits made on equity shares and equity mutual funds sold 1 year after the date of purchase, are exempt from tax, so no TDS applies. For short-term capital gains however, i.e. profits on sales within one year of purchase date, a TDS of 15% applies.

Long-term capital gains which occur from the sale of debt mutual funds, or corporate debentures, attract TDS at 10 per cent. Short-term capital gains are currently subject to a TDS of 30 per cent.

When it comes to capital gains on assets such as real estate or gold, the long-term capital gains TDS rate is 20% and the short-term capital gain TDS rate is 30%.

TDS on the sale of property in India

While banks and other institutions deduct TDS automatically and submit tax amount deducted to the tax authorities, there are cases where this is not possible, for example, when a house is sold. In such cases, the buyer is responsible for ensuring that TDS is taken and sent to the authorities.

Tax deduction in the form of TDS deduction, applies to all sorts of property sold in India other than agricultural land, if the sale amount is more than Rupees 50 lakh. As per the Indian Income Tax Act, tax must be deducted at source by the buyer of a property from payments made to a seller.

The rate of tax deduction if seller is a resident of India is 1%. If the seller is a non-resident the TDS applicable rate is 20% for long term capital gains or as per applicable tax slab, for short term capital gain. A credit for the TDS deducted can be claimed by the seller by filling a tax return.

Buyer of a property is exempt from the requirement to procure TAN which otherwise is mandatory in all cases where a person deducts tax (TDS). Buyer of the property is required to submit the money deducted as TDS to the tax department within 7 days. Notification to the income-tax department of property TDS deduction is done by the seller on Form 26QB.

Notification as well as payment can be done online from the Indian tax department website: https://www.tin-nsdl.com/

TDS on rental income in India

TDS on rental income also comes under the other income category which calls for TDS @ 30%. The tenants in such cases are supposed to apply for a Tax Deduction Account Number (TAN), deduct TDS from the rental amount and send the tax collected to the tax authorities. The tenant should issue a TDS certificate to the landlord.

In cases where income exceeds Rupees 10 lakh, a surcharge of 10 per cent is generally applicable on the TDS. Furthermore, an educational cess of 3 per cent also applies to all TDS.

Refund of TDS deducted on bank interest

NRIs, who have income in India that is below the tax free allowance, can claim a refund for the TDS deducted. Most non-residents who have bank accounts in India would probably qualify for a refund of either a partial or all of the TDS they were charged. However, not many NRIs bother to claim TDS deducted because to claim a refund, a tax return must be filed in India.

Tax tips for US Citizens living in India

Citizens of the United States who hold OCI status and have relocated to India, as well as those who have business interests in India, should ensure that they continue to comply with IRS laws. There appears to be an extra push in the United States to recover taxes from their citizens, who may have assets and undeclared income abroad.

U.S. Citizens and resident aliens are subject to U.S. taxes even if they reside abroad. Their worldwide income is taxable in the United States.

Who is a considered a 'Resident Alien' in USA

If one of the following two conditions apply to you then you are considered to be a resident alien

1. Have a green card or had a green card in the last calendar year
2. Have been in the United States for more than 31 days during the current year AND been in the U.S. for at least 183 days over a three year period which includes the current year.

U.S. tax liability basis

Contrary to the Indian tax system which is based on residency, The United States tax system is based on one's citizenship as well as residence.

As a U.S. citizen, no matter what part of the world you go to, the chances are, you cannot escape U.S. taxes. The penalties levied by the IRS are also severe and enough to force just about everyone, to stay in compliance of U.S. tax laws.

As a U.S. expatriate residing in India, you still owe U.S. taxes each year on your worldwide income. U.S. Permanent Residents (green card holders) as well as U.S. Citizens must report each year their income earned anywhere in the world.

Penalties for not filing U.S. taxes

Failure to comply with U.S. tax filing laws may possibly result in civil penalties, criminal penalties or both. By combating international tax evasion the IRS claims to have collected 2.7 billion dollars, since 2009, from thousands of U.S. taxpayers. *(IR-2011-94, Sept. 15, 2011)*

According to an article, published in the 'Wall Street Journal' (March 10, 2011) growing numbers of Americans who live overseas are renouncing U.S. citizenship because of mounting tax and reporting obligations.

What is worldwide income for U.S. Citizens

Worldwide income means that your U.S. income tax return must include:

- Foreign dividends
- Rental Income Earned Abroad
- Foreign pension income
- Foreign capital gains or losses on stocks, bonds, real estate
- Foreign royalties
- All other foreign income

Be aware that if you aren't filing your U.S. tax return, the statute of limitations on tax collections will not run out and, your tax return obligation will continue to grow greater as each year passes. [More info on statute of limitations on page 118]

The U.S. has income tax treaties with several countries, including India. Now, both the IRS and the foreign taxing authorities have the capability to easily exchange information on their citizens living in the other country. The IRS had in 2009 offered an amnesty program offering lower penalties for those who declared their foreign bank assets. Approximately 15,000 accounts held abroad were uncovered in 2009.

Those who voluntarily disclose their foreign bank accounts and assets could receive reduced penalties, preventing large fines and possible jail sentences.

IRS news release in Hindi

On February 8, 2011 the IRS issued a news release in the Hindi language, perhaps to encourage U.S. Citizens of Indian origin to comply and not risk the possibility of penalties. You can view the IRS Hindi news release on the IRS website, or access it from our website NriInformation.com by visiting: http://nriinformation.com/nri_guide/index_htm_files/irs_taxes_hindi.pdf

Filing Requirements for U.S. Citizens in India

The rules for filing U.S. tax returns remain the same for U.S. citizens and resident aliens, regardless of whether they are residing abroad or in the United States.

Those who hold 'Green Cards' are resident aliens, and the same tax rules that apply to U.S. citizens generally also apply to green card holders. Rules for filing income, estate, gift tax returns and for paying estimated tax, are the same whether you are in the United States, India, or any other part of the world.

Generally your income, filing status and age determine whether you must file an income tax return. The requirement for filing a return in the year 2015 (2014 year income) is If your gross income is above the threshold for your age and filing status set by the IRS.

Self Employed Persons

Those who are self-employed are required to file a U.S. income tax return if they had $400 or more of net earnings from self-employment, regardless of their age. Net earnings from self-employment include income earned both in a foreign country and in the United States.

Minimum Income Requirement to file U.S. Tax

The minimum income required to file a tax return for a Tax Year in the United States depends on your income, age, and filing status. The minimum income levels for the various filing statuses are shown on the next page.

♦ ♦ ♦

Minimum income required to file tax return for Tax Year 2014

Filing Status*	Amount
Single	$10,150
65 or older	$11,700
Head of household	$13,050
65 or older	$14,600
Qualifying widow(er)	$16,350
65 or older with dependent children	$17,550
Married filing jointly 65 or older	$22,700
Not living with spouse at end of year	$3,950
One spouse 65 or older	$21,500
Both spouses 65 or older	$22,700
Married filing separately	$3,950

**(Source: IRS Publication 54, Tax Guide for U.S. Citizens and Resident Aliens Abroad.)*

The IRS has an Interactive Tax Assistant (ITA) that can be used to determine whether an individual needs to file a tax return. ITA can be accessed from https://www.irs.gov

US Citizens living abroad benefit by filling taxes

The tax agreement between India and the United States may reduce or eliminate any double taxation of your income. The IRS allows credits for foreign income taxes you pay while living outside the United States. These credits may help offset any U.S. tax you might owe on your Indian income. However, to claim the credit you must file your U.S. tax return, every year.

Not filling your US taxes can only increase your tax liability. Suppose you live in India for 5 years and then return to the United States. The IRS may question your failure to file returns for the past five years, in such cases; they normally make assessments based on their best estimate of your income. The interest and penalties on any old tax amounts accumulates rapidly. In a few years you may end up owing a lot more than the original taxes owed.

Voluntarily filing as opposed to the IRS coming to you, can make a big difference in how you will get treated if any penalties are assessed, for failing to file U.S. tax returns.

New foreign account reporting requirements are being phased in over the next few years, making it even tougher to hide income in foreign countries. The IRS is now focusing on banks and bankers worldwide in an effort to find U.S. taxpayers who may be hiding assets overseas.

U.S. Citizens having bank account in India

Citizens of the United States, as well as those who are deemed to be U.S. residents, are required to report foreign bank accounts to the IRS if they meet the defined guidelines.

Reporting foreign bank accounts is called FBAR and such reports are submitted on Form TD F 90-22.1. More information on FBAR is provided below.

Reporting foreign bank accounts (FBAR)

FBAR stands for 'Foreign Bank Account Report'. It is a report of foreign bank and financial accounts held by U.S. Citizens or US resident aliens abroad. If you are a U.S. citizen or green card holder who has bank accounts abroad, you must file a FBAR report on Form 90-22.1 if the aggregate value of the accounts exceeds $10,000, during a calendar year.

The FBAR is due by June 30th of the year following the year that the account holder meets the $10,000 threshold.

The threshold would be the aggregate of all your accounts abroad. Suppose you have three accounts, then if the total amount of all three accounts added, goes over $10,000 FBAR reporting is required.

Effective July 1, 2013, the FBAR must be filed electronically.

FBAR filling for OCI holder residing in India

U.S. citizens and residents who have financial accounts in India, such as NRO, NRE accounts, where the value of the account exceeds the equivalent amount of US$ 10,000 at any time during a calendar year, must file a 'Report of Foreign Bank and Financial Accounts' (FBAR) on form number TD F 90-22. FBAR is also referred to as FinCEN 114.

Some examples regarding FBAR are provided for clarification purposes are provided on the next page.

Example1: *(When living abroad)*

Mr. Raja, a U.S. Citizen having OCI is living in India and has a bank account in India. Let's assume that the current balance in his account is of Rs. 6, 41,000.

Using the conversion rate of Rupee to US dollar @ 60 the total amount in Mr. Raja's account is equal to US$ 10,683. As this amount is over the US$ 10,000 threshold, Mr. Raj is required to file a FBAR report.

Example2: *(When living in USA)*

Mr. Sharma, a U.S. citizen is living in New York. He has a bank account in India that has more than the equivalent of US$ 10,000 in the account. Even though Mr. Sharma continues to live in the United States, he is still required to file a FBAR report.

Example3: *(Multiple foreign accounts)*

Shreya a green card holder has three NRI accounts in India. Her account balances when converted to US$ are:

1. *SBI bank $2500*
2. *Axis bank $5600*
3. *HDFC bank $2100*

Total of all three accounts works out to US$ 10,200. As this is over the FBAR threshold she must file FBAR report.

Note: Even where the threshold is not reached for FBAR reporting. Account holders are required to declare any interest income received when filing U.S. taxes.

Keep track of interest credited to your account to ensure you know when your account total goes over $10,000.

Failure to file foreign bank accounts report

Failing to file an FBAR when required to do so may possibly result in civil penalties and/or criminal penalties. Failure to file FBAR in time can lead to penalties of $10,000 for each non-willful violation. In case the IRS determines the failure to file as being a willful violation, then the penalty imposed by the IRS can be the greater of $100,000 or 50% of the amount in the account, for each violation. If you have questions regarding FBAR, contact the IRS at FBARquestions@irs.gov.

Statute of limitations for US Taxes

A statute of limitations is a law which sets a certain time period after which a party is barred from enforcing their rights. As far as IRS audit is concerned, they have three years from the time you file to decide whether to audit or not. Once the three years have expired then the statute of limitations has run out.

Suppose you are now living in India and file a US tax return every year. In most situations the statute of limitations for IRS audits will expire after three years and the IRS normally, cannot go back to audit any returns you filed three years ago. On the other hand, if you don't file a tax return the statute of limitations will never run out.

Even if you don't have income, you may want to consider filling a tax return every year, just so the statute of limitations for that filling year runs out.

Note: While the statute of limitations runs out in three years for IRS, kindly note that the three years can be doubled to six years if when filling their tax return:

1. A person omitted more than 25% of their income
2. Failed to report more than $5000 of foreign income

Advantages to filling U.S. Taxes from India

In addition to being compliant with U.S. laws, there are a few other advantages to filing taxes from abroad that you should know about. Several income tax benefits might apply if you meet certain requirements while living abroad. However you can only claim these benefits if you file your taxes in a timely manner.

Foreign Earned Income Exclusion

If you have moved to India and live there now:

- As a full time resident for a full calendar year or
- Live there for 330 days out of any consecutive 12-month period

You can exclude up to $100,800 of earned income for the year 2015 when filing your U.S. Income Tax. If you are married and both of you earn income while residing abroad, you can also exclude up to the same amount from your spouse's income and save even more on your U.S. tax obligations.

These exclusions can only be claimed by filling a tax return in the applicable year. Remember, foreign earned income exclusion applies only if a tax return is filed and the income is reported.

Note: Applies only to **earned income**. Other income such as interest income, pensions, dividends, capital gains etc. cannot be excluded under 'Foreign Earned Income Exclusion'.

The Foreign Account Tax Compliance Act (FATCA)

The Foreign Account Tax Compliance Act (FATCA) was enacted in 2010. FATCA affects U.S. tax payers who hold foreign assets that exceed US$50,000. The IRS requires Information about such assets on a new form (Form 8938). This form must be attached to the taxpayer's annual return. FATCA reporting applies for assets held in taxable years beginning after March 18, 2010.

FATCA Reporting - How it works

There are two reporting requirements under FATCA. One is for individuals and the other for financial institutions where U.S. citizens or green card holders have accounts.

Individuals holding financial assets in India or anywhere else abroad are required to report those assets to the IRS using Form 8938 'Specified Foreign Financial Assets' attached to their annual U.S. income tax return.

Indian financial institutions such as banks are required under FATCA rules to report the names, addresses, tax identification numbers, account numbers and balances of each account holder who is a U.S. citizen or a green card holder.

FATCA India – USA Reporting

The Indian Government signed an Inter-Governmental Agreement with the United States on 9 July 2015, to implement the Foreign Account Tax Compliance Act (FATCA) in India.

Under the inter-governmental agreement, Indian financial

institutions would provide information about bank accounts of US citizens and residents to the Government of India, which will then send this information to the U.S. Internal Revenue Service.

Likewise, the IRS would provide information to the Indian Government about Indian citizens having financial accounts & assets in the United States.

This exchange of information is scheduled to begin on 30 September 2015.

IRS Reporting Importance for U.S. NRIs

It does not get any easier for US citizens who live abroad. The IRS appears to be moving to stricter enforcement methods to track down those who may owe taxes. FATCA goes in to full swing as of September 30, 2015 when both IRS and the Indian government will exchange information under FATCA. The IRS will have the facility to quickly cross check filings by financial institutions to verify that individuals have complied by filling Form 8938 that is required under FATCA.

U.S. NRIs who have foreign financial assets greater than US $50,000, must report their income under FATCA using Form 8938 to stay in compliance of U.S. tax laws.

UK Citizens living in India

Tax liability in the United Kingdom depends on your residential status for taxation purposes. To limit their tax liability, UK residents who return to India for long term settlement, should take steps to let the tax authorities know they are leaving UK.

Tax tips for UK Expats

Persons of Indian Origin (PIO) holding UK passports and living in India, should be aware that those who are deemed to have UK residence for tax purposes, are normally liable to be taxed on their worldwide income.

Worldwide Income would mean that they would be required to pay tax on:

- ✓ Income which arises in the UK
- ✓ Income which arises outside the UK
- ✓ Gains which accrue on the disposal of assets anywhere in the world.

Having UK non-resident status exempts a person from paying tax on their foreign income in UK. Generally UK non-residents only have to pay tax in UK on their UK income.

UK residents who have their permanent home outside UK are known as 'Non-domiciled' residents and they may not have to pay tax in UK on their foreign income. Special rules apply to non-domiciled UK resident's foreign income and capital gains. They have an option to use either the **arising basis** of taxation or the **remittance basis.**

If Remittance basis is selected, then UK tax will be payable on:

- Any foreign income that is brought into or sent to UK
- Income and gains that arise in UK

Readers should be aware that there is a possibility of an individual being classified as having residency of two countries at the same time. In such cases normally the provisions of the DTAA would apply. UK expats should seek clarification and guidance on their residency status issues from their accountants to minimize their tax liabilities.

Who is a resident or non-resident in the UK

Normally, if you live or work in UK you are a resident. To claim non-resident status you must live in the UK for less than 183 days. However, even if you are in the UK for less than 183 days, you could still be treated as a resident for the year.

Physical presence in the country is **not the only factor** used to decide if a person is a non-resident for taxation purposes.

On the other hand, physical presence in the UK for 183 days or more WILL make you a resident for tax purposes.

Who is automatically considered UK resident

You are considered to be a resident if:

- You spent 183 or more days in the UK in the tax year. **Or**
- Your home was in the UK - you either owned, rented or lived in it for at least 91 days in total and spent at least 30 days there in the tax year. **Or**
- Work full time in UK

Automatically considered UK non-resident

You are considered to be non-resident if:

- You left the UK for full-time work abroad. [more than 35 hours a week average over the tax year]
- You spend less than 16 days in the UK.
- You were **not** UK resident in the previous three tax years and spend less than 46 days in the UK

Being treated as a UK resident can have a big impact on your UK tax bill. OCI holders in UK who are relocating to India can take steps to minimize their UK tax liability by declaring their non-residency to the UK tax authorities. This should ideally be done before they leave or as soon as possible if you have already left UK.

How to declare Non- Residency in UK

One of the first step to adjusting your residency status for tax purposes is to notify HM Revenue and Customs (HMRC) of your intention to leave the UK. This can be done by submitting a duly filled 'Form P85' to HMRC. Form P85 should be available from HMRC, a sample of this form can also be viewed at our website by visiting the link: http://nriinformation.com/form_p85.pdf

How not to lose your non-resident status in UK

Once you become a non-resident for tax purposes, you will not be taxed on your income that is derived outside UK. However it's important that you take steps to ensure that you do not lose your non-resident status accidently. Keep track of the time you spend in UK on visits as this can affect your residency.

A person can become a resident for tax purposes when one of the following applies:

- ✓ If in any year, you spend in excess of 183 days in the UK or
- ✓ Spend over 90 days in the UK on average over the last four tax years; you will be classed as a UK resident.

Most people seem to remember the 183 day rule, however many are probably not aware of the second condition (or fail to keep track of their visits to UK) and end up spending more than an average of 90 days in UK over the last four tax years.

When this happens, you will be classed as UK resident from the fifth year, and this would put your worldwide income at risk of being taxed in UK.

Maintain UK Non-resident status – Save on UK taxes

UK citizens who are not domiciled in the UK, and/or not ordinarily resident in the UK can take advantage of special rules that apply to foreign income and gains. These rules allow them to pay UK tax only on the amount of their foreign income and gains that they take back or remit to the UK.

To avoid paying taxes on your worldwide income in the UK, all social and family ties with the UK need to be severed. Some of the things that you should consider:

- ➢ If possible, avoid visiting the UK in the first year of non-residency.
- ➢ Keep future visits to UK at an absolute minimum

- Remember that spending over 90 days in the UK on average over the last four years will make you a resident. Plan any visit to UK keeping this in mind.

In the event a person loses their non-resident status in UK and their worldwide income becomes taxable. The Double Tax Avoidance Agreement (DTAA) would provide relief to some extent minimize their tax liability.

Canadian citizens in India

Canadian residents are subject to Canadian income tax on their worldwide income. Canadians of Indian origin who are planning to move back to India, should ensure that they adjust their residency status in Canada, before leaving. This way, they can avoid paying taxes on their foreign income in Canada.

Steps to take when leaving Canada permanently

The information mentioned below is for Canadian citizens and not intended for PR card holders. According to Canadian rules, PR card holders must live in Canada for at least two years in a five-year period. If they live outside of Canada for longer periods they risk losing their permanent resident status.

If you are a Canadian citizen and wish to move out of Canada there are some steps that can be taken to become non-resident in Canada for tax purposes.

- Notify Revenue Canada of your intent to leave, and give them the date of your intended departure. Chances are that your departure date may become the day you are considered to have become a non-resident.
- Those who receive credits such as GST or HST, Child tax benefits etc. should notify the appropriate authorities of their intended departure. Once you leave Canada, you will no longer qualify for these benefits. In case you do receive a cheque for such payments, make sure you don't cash it. Notify CRA of such payments so that they can update the appropriate records.

- Take steps to close your bank accounts, credit cards, your provincial health card, etc. It is to your benefit to make sure that you show that you are indeed breaking all ties with Canada and are moving abroad either permanently or indefinitely.

To assess the tax obligations of Canadians living abroad the Canadian Revenue Agency (CRA) uses "residency status" as the criteria.

Residency for tax purposes does not merely refer to where you physically live; actually residency status has no effect on citizenship or immigration. To determine residency for tax purposes, the CRA will look into what connections you have to Canada.

The CRA has four categories to classify Expatriate Canadians for tax purposes:

- Factual Resident
- Deemed Resident
- Non-Resident
- Deemed Non-Resident

Factual residents

You are considered to be a factual resident of Canada, if you keep significant residential ties in Canada, while living or travelling outside the country. Those classified as factual residents are considered to be a resident of Canada for income tax purposes.

Deemed Resident

This classification usually would refer to a person who even though they do not maintain residential ties to Canada, they file Canadian tax returns. An example of this category would be government employees who are stationed abroad.

Non-Residents

Those who have no ties with Canada will usually fall under non-resident classification. Such people would have severed just about all their residential ties to Canada and live abroad permanently. Those classified as non-residents for tax purposes in Canada are not taxed on their worldwide income. They are taxed only on income from Canadian sources.

Deemed Non-Resident

A person who is a resident of a country that has a tax treaty with Canada is usually deemed as a non-resident and is subject to the same rules as those in the non-resident category. Since Canada does have a tax treaty with India, OCI card holders who start living in India may fall under this category. As a deemed non-resident, only income from your Canadian sources is taxed.

Australian Citizens living in India

Australians can be taxed on their worldwide income unless they become non-residents for tax purposes. Those who are considered as non-residents for tax purposes in Australia are taxed only on income that is derived from Australian sources.

Normally if you leave Australia permanently, for tax purposes you are treated as a non-resident from the date of your departure. Persons of Indian origin from Australia, who plan on settling in India, can take advantage their non-resident status to avoid additional tax liabilities in Australia. Once they are non-residents, there is no requirement to declare their Indian income in Australia.

Australian citizens who are considered non-residents for taxation purposes, are required to pay taxes in Australia on all income derived from Australian sources, e.g. bank interest, dividends, rental income, etc.

Australian OCI holders have an advantage over U.S. OCI holders because:

- U.S. OCI holders who move back to India are required to file taxes in USA and declare any income they earn in India or anywhere else in the world.
- Australian OCI holders who decided to move back to India are not required to file taxes in Australia to declare their income in India or anywhere else in the world. They are taxed only on their Australian income and required to file an Australian tax return only if they have Australian income.

At some point of time, Australian citizens residing in India will also lose their 'Not Ordinarily Resident' (NOR) tax category status. Their worldwide income would then become taxable in India. However, as India and Australia, have a tax treaty between them, Australians living in India will get relief from dual taxation. When filing their tax return in India, they will receive a credit for any taxes they've already paid in Australia.

Points to Remember:

- If you are an Australian citizen, resident in Australia, your worldwide income is taxable in Australia.
- If you leave Australia temporarily and do not set up a permanent home in another country, you remain an Australian resident for tax purposes and your global income is taxable.
- If you leave Australia permanently, you are not treated as an Australian resident for tax purposes from the date of your departure.
- An Australian citizen with OCI, if they move to India and become non-residents in Australia, then any income they earn in India is exempt from taxes in Australia. The only taxes they would have to pay in Australia would be on income that is derived from within Australia.

OCI holders should keep in mind that even though they might be treated as non-residents from the day they left Australia permanently with the intention of living in India, in case they spend more than 183 days in Australia, either continuously or intermittently, they may become a resident of Australia for tax purposes.

Property in India - Information

Persons of Indian origin (PIO) can buy residential or commercial property in India, without any prior approval from the Reserve Bank of India (RBI). The RBI has given general permission to allowing NRIs and PIO to acquire residential or commercial properties in India. Provided they meet the following conditions:

- They are NOT citizens of any of the following countries:
  - Pakistan
  - Bangladesh
  - Sri Lanka
  - Afghanistan
  - China
  - Iran
  - Nepal
  - Bhutan
- They held an Indian passport before acquiring foreign citizenship OR they themselves (or either their father or grandfather) are a citizen of India by virtue of the Constitution of India or the Citizenship Act. 1955
- RBI general permission does not apply for the purchase of agricultural land/plantation property/farm house in India.

While citizens of Pakistan, Bangladesh, Sri Lanka, Afghanistan, China, Iran, Nepal or Bhutan cannot acquire or transfer immovable property in India without the prior permission of the Reserve Bank of India. They can lease property for a maximum of five years.

Kindly note: foreign nationals of countries (not on the

prohibited country list) who can purchase property in India without RBI permission, can do so only if they are of Indian origin. [*Notification No FEMA 21/2000-RB dated May 3, 2000]*

For those who meet this requirement, there are no restrictions on the number of residential or commercial properties that can be purchased. The general permission given by the RBI does NOT apply for purchasing agricultural land, plantation property, or a farm house in India. Citizens of Pakistan, Bangladesh, Sri Lanka, Afghanistan, China, Iran, Nepal and Bhutan, are not permitted to purchase property in India without prior approval, of the Reserve Bank of India. In case citizens of these countries already own property in India, they cannot transfer such properties without prior RBI permission.

Purchase of property by foreign companies

Foreign companies in India, who have been authorized to open a branch or project office in India, are allowed to acquire any immovable property in India, where such property is necessary for (or related to) carrying on their business activity.

RBI notification not required to purchase property

NRIs and PIO, who purchase residential or commercial property in India under the general permission granted by the RBI, are not required to file any documents with the Reserve Bank of India.

Property purchase by foreigners

Foreign nationals of non-India origin are not authorized to

purchase property in India. In case a foreigner who is living in India as a resident wishes to purchase property, they require prior RBI approval.

Gifting property to NRIs

Any person residing in India, or an NRI/PIO, can gift property they own to any other Indian citizen, NRI or PIO. This applies only to residential or commercial property.

Property gifting restrictions

- Agricultural land, plantation or farm house property in India cannot be gifted to NRIs or PIO.
- Property located in India, cannot be gifted to a foreign national of non-Indian origin.

Foreigners require RBI permission to gift property

A foreign national of non-Indian origin requires the prior approval of the Reserve Bank before they can gift any kind of property located in India that they own.

Tax on Gifts

As per current rules there is no gift tax on gifts valued up to Rupees 50,000. Any gift up to this value can be given to a relative or non-relative and no tax applies.

Gifts valued at over Rupees 50,000 to Non-Relative

In case an individual receives cash or non-cash gifts from someone other than close relatives and the amount is in excess of Rs 50,000 in a year, then the entire amount of the gift received will be treated as the individual's income and must be included under 'Income from other sources'. If it does not exceed Rs 50,000, it will not be treated as income.

Example: Raj gifts his friend Neha Rupees 51,000. Since gifted amount is over Rupees 50,000 the entire amount of Rupees 51,000 must be shown as income from other sources by Neha on her tax return. She will be taxed according to the slab that would apply according to her income.

- In case the gifted amount was not more than Rupees 50,000, then no tax would apply.

Gifts to close relatives

Gifts in excess of Rupees 50,000 to close relatives are exempt. There is no tax liability if gifts are between close relatives. The definition of a relative is provided in section 56 clause (vi) of sub-section (2) of the I-T Act.

For a gift in India to be tax free when the value is over Rupees 50,000, the relative should be the individuals:

- ✓ Spouse
- ✓ Brother or Sister
- ✓ Brother or sister of either spouse
- ✓ Brother or sister of either parents of the individual or
- ✓ Any hereditary ascendant of either spouse

When is gifted property taxed in India?

Gifts over Rs. 50,000, received from people who are not considered as relatives are taxed. Normally the person receiving the gift is required to pay taxes on such gifts. Since we are talking of property gifts here, the fair market value of the gifted property is considered the amount to have been gifted.

While there is a limit of Rs. 50,000 for gifts to non-relatives, there is no limit when gifts are given to relatives. They would be tax free. NRIs can gift any amount to a person who qualifies as a relative and such gifts would be tax free.

Gift of money to cover black money

NRIs should exercise care if they are asked to give gift cheque to resident Indians in exchange of cash money. This is normally done in an effort to turn black money around. Such transactions though they appear to be harmless, are illegal.

Example: Promila, a person of Indian origin, while visiting India is asked to give a cheque of Rs. 50,000 to an Indian resident, who would pay her Rs.60, 000 in cash. While Promila may not be aware of it, she is breaking the law.

The tax authorities are aware of such schemes where residents try to turn black money that they cannot account for, as money given to them as a gift. NRIs should naturally refrain from such activities as they are illegal and can result in problems and penalties.

When gifts are given, be aware that proper documentation is required to prove the gifts received are genuine and the gift giver has the capacity to give such gifts.

Wealth tax in India abolished 2015-2016 FY

Wealth tax was payable in India if your assets (net wealth)

exceeded Rs. 30 lakh. The tax rate for wealth tax was 1% on the amount by which your net wealth exceeded Rs. 30 lakhs. A vast number of people however were not considered to have assets of Rs. 30 lakh due to exemptions of what constituted wealth.

The Wealth Tax Act provided for exemption of one house from tax. One house was exempt regardless of the value of the house. If you had just one house, even if it is worth Rs.100 crore, it was exempt from wealth tax.

Finance Minister of India Mr. Jaitley announced in the 2015 budget that starting the financial year 2015-2016 onwards, Wealth Tax has been completely removed.

♦ ♦ ♦

Inheriting property by NRI

Inheriting property located in India, by a non-resident can sometimes be a confusing task to handle, particularly for persons who have been away from India for a long time. NRIs who inherit property may find themselves faced with questions such as:

- Who can inherit property in India?
- Legality of ownership
- Taxes to be paid?
- Sale of the inherited property
- Repatriation of the sale proceeds, etc.

Who can inherit immoveable property in India

There are some instances where Indian residents tell their non-resident relatives that they cannot inherit property in India, as they are foreigners. However, this is not true.

Anyone can inherit property in India, whether they are persons of Indian origin or not. Even foreign nationals, who may have not even visited India, can inherit property located in India.

NRIs can inherit not only residential and commercial property but also plantation and agricultural lands. Even though agricultural land and plantation property cannot be acquired by NRIs by way of purchase or gift, they can legally inherit it.

The only exceptions here are:

1. Foreigners of most countries can inherit property in India without any RBI permission. However, citizens of Pakistan,

Bangladesh, Sri Lanka, Afghanistan, China, Iran, Nepal and Bhutan must seek prior approval from the Reserve Bank of India.

2. In cases where the property is being inherited by a person who is resident outside India, there is a condition that the property must have been acquired, in accordance with the foreign exchange (FEMA) applicable laws that were in effect when the property was purchased.

Clarification: *A person who bought property in contravention of the foreign exchange law in force or FEMA regulations, applicable at the time of acquisition of the property would not have owned the property legally and hence cannot pass it on by way of inheritance to anyone.*

Tax when inheriting property

Inheritance tax is commonly known as the Estate Tax/Duty in India. This type of tax was introduced in the year 1953, and was abolished in 1985, when Mr. V P Singh was the Finance Minister. Currently when inheriting property, there is no inheritance tax in India. Capital gains tax may apply when inherited property is sold.

Sale of properties owned by NRIs

When NRIs or foreigners want to sell their properties that are located in India, there are some guidelines set by the Reserve Bank of India that must be followed.

Depending on the seller and purchaser's status in India, RBI permission may or may not be required, to sell property located in India.

Some of the RBI rules regarding sale of property by non-residents are shown in the table:

NRI Selling residential/commercial property

Seller	Purchaser	Remarks
NRI	Can Sell to anyone	No permission required to sell
PIO	Person resident in India or NRI who has Indian citizenship	No permission required to sell
PIO	PIO	Prior approval of Reserve Bank of India is required to sell.
Foreign nationals of non-Indian origin	Person resident in India or an NRI/PIO	Reserve Bank of India approval is required

Sale of agricultural land in India

Seller	Remarks
NRI / PIO	Can sell agricultural land /plantation property/farm house to a person **resident** in India who is also a **citizen** of India. No RBI permission is required.
Foreigner non-Indian origin	Prior approval of Reserve Bank required to sell agricultural land/plantation property/ farm house in India

Mortgaging property held in India

NRI/PIO can mortgage commercial or residential properties they hold in India. No approval from the Reserve Bank of India is required if they obtain mortgages from authorized dealers in India.

Prior approval of the Reserve Bank is required if NRIs wish to mortgage property they hold in India, to a party abroad.

Paying abroad for property located in India

Non-residents may be asked to accept payment abroad for a property they have sold in India. To some NRIs this may seem like an ideal situation, as they would not have to worry about repatriation of the sale proceeds from India. This type of dealing is specifically not permitted by the authorities in India.

This is also important from a legal point of view, as the registration and transfer of ownership of property that is located in India, must be recorded in India. Even if both seller and buyer are non-residents, the payment must be made in India.

Payments for property purchase by NRIs

NRIs when purchasing property in India should make payments for property purchases only through legal banking channels. Money laundering is a concern in all countries and India is no exception.

When purchasing property in India, there is a tendency by some, to pay a portion of the purchase price in cash and the rest by banking channels, to save on registration fee, stamp duty etc.

Cash payments should be avoided when buying property in India. Saving a small sum of money on registration costs is not worth the risk. Make payments only via legal banking methods. Disputes can arise at any time between purchasers and buyers and having a proper record of all dealings is important for both buyer and seller.

NRIs also have the option to purchase commercial or residential properties in India, by obtaining a mortgage from authorized dealers such as banks, in India.

Turning legal money into illegal money!

Many people do this and don't even realize it. Non-residents, who accept cash when selling their properties, may be accumulating what is known as black money. This type of money is accumulated by illegal activities such as, bribes, tax evasion etc. If a purchaser does not want to declare the true value of the property they are buying, they many insist on paying partially in cash.

The reason they may normally give:

- ✓ They want to save money on registration/stamp duty.
- ✓ They point out that the seller will save on capital gains!

Normally, the reason is that the amount of money they want to pay in cash is money, they cannot account for.

Suppose you accept such a proposal when selling your property, and take cash for part of the deal. The registration of the property is done and the cash payment is excluded from the price of the property. In such a scenario, what has happened is that you have relieved the purchaser of cash money that he could not account for. Now you have money that you cannot account for. Some of the problems these types of transactions can create for NRIs are:

1. They are stuck with money they cannot account for.
2. They can't deposit large sums of cash in their bank accounts as cash deposits over Rupees 50,000 may be automatically reported to the tax authorities by banks.
3. It's easy to repatriate the sale proceeds of property these days, provided it can be verified that the money has indeed come from the sale of property. In this case the cash part cannot be repatriated.

When selling their property in India, NRIs should avoid cash transactions. Accepting payments by legal banking channels will not only keep you in compliance of the law, but also make it possible to legally repatriate the sale proceeds of your property.

Purchasing Property in India

More and more non-resident Indians now holding foreign passports are purchasing property in India. While every non-resident would have their own reasons of purchasing property in India, some of the common reasons are:

1. Their desire to return to India sometime in the future.
2. For investment purposes.
3. To have a place in India when visiting.

While purchasing property in India is a wise decision, the last thing non-residents want on their hands is a legal dispute involving property in India. Courts in India are pretty slow and cases can drag on for tens of years. Non-residents who purchase property in India, should be extra careful when signing contracts and giving deposits. Seek the help of a lawyer to verify documentation.

Buying land in India

When buying land, take every step possible to ascertain ownership of the land. This is no easy task for non-residents. The problem with land purchases in India is, the verification of ownership of the land being purchased.

While India is gradually moving in the direction of computerizing property records, this facility is not widely available yet. Most records need to be verified manually and such searches are often time consuming.

NRIs should always seek the help of a lawyer, when purchasing land in India. When purchasing land, here are some of the things that non-resident property purchasers should consider:

- Ownership record check
- Getting an 'Encumbrance Certificate'
- Getting a 'Release Certificate'

Land ownership record check

Only the rightful owner has the right to sell their property, ensuring that you are dealing with the legal owner, is the number one factor when buying property. Get a check done of the ownership records of the property for at least the past 30 years. This should show you the list of all transactions associated with the property during this period. Don't simply accept the documents given to you by the seller on face value. Have your own search and verification done at the appropriate registration office.

Encumbrance Certificate

The current owner may have pledged the property to a bank to get a loan. The purpose of an encumbrance certificate is to find out whether the property being purchased has a mortgage/charge on it. The encumbrance certificate will show all the transactions registered, relating to a particular property for a specified period.

Depending on which state in India you are purchasing property, you may also hear of 'Non-Encumbrance certificate' or 'Nil-Encumbrance certificate'. The purpose of these documents is normally the same.

How to obtain encumbrance certificate

Encumbrance certificates, are obtained from the sub-registrar's office, where the deed for the land has been registered. The procedure involves:

- Submitting an application to get encumbrance certificate to the sub-registrar's office, under whose jurisdiction the property is located.
- Providing details of the property such as the correct survey number etc. for which the certificate is required. You should get this information form the seller.
- Providing proof of residence.
- Paying the appropriate fee. This is based on the number of years you wish to get the certificate for. Request for at least 30 years is recommended. Have heard of people doing searches for the past 100 years also!

Encumbrance certificate is issued by the Sub-Registrar and should help you find information about the property such as:

- Documents registered in respect of the property.
- The parties to the property deed.
- Nature of charges created if any, amounts secured or transacted in respect of the property.
- Title information, registered details and document identifying numbers etc.

While encumbrance certificate is an important document when purchasing property in India, there are some limitations, on the information that these certificates provide.

NRIs should not solely rely on information provided on an encumbrance certificate.

Limitations of Encumbrance Certificates

These certificates are issued for a specific period of time, and fee is charged accordingly. It does not cover any period prior to or following the period mentioned. Any encumbrance, prior or later than the dates for which the certificate is issued, would not be known. This is the reason; information should be request for a longer period of time.

Generally, the encumbrance certificate issued by the sub-registrar is based exclusively on the documents registered with the registrar's office. Any document that has not been registered will not be mentioned on the certificate you receive.

In case you are wondering what type of documents may not be registered with the registrar, regarding a property? Here is an example:

- Suppose the property is leased, any lease that is for a period of less than one year, does not have to be registered with the registrar.
- Testamentary documents are not required to be registered.
- In a case where a lender may loan money, after taking custody of the original documents of the property. The lender may not register the loan, thinking that the property cannot be sold, as long as they have the original documents.

Release Certificate for a property

In the event a property was pledged by the seller in the past, even though the loans have been repaid, ask the seller to provide you with a release certificate. This would be a document issued by the bank that provided the loan, confirming that all loan payments have been made and there are no outstanding dues associated with the property.

Benefit of getting property loan in India

If you are buying property in India, then perhaps you may want to consider applying for a loan. Even if you don't need the money, there may be a benefit in getting one for a short time. Banks are in the money business and believe it or not, do their homework when it comes to giving out loans.

A good credit rating is a major factor when banks in western countries approve loans. In India the majority of loans are based on collateral. Before a bank will loan you money to purchase property in India, they will verify the particulars of the property for which the money will be loaned by them.

Banks have professionals working for them who are pretty good at assessing property values. They are usually also aware of builder's reputations in the market, as they deal with these issues on an ongoing basis.

When banks loan money for a property, they will scrutinize the builder's land ownership, building permits records etc. diligently before advancing money.

Even though a purchaser's lawyer would do the required search, a second opinion is always welcome when trying to verify property ownership records in India.

Consider Ready to Move in Property

Considering the problems faced by many purchasers of under construction homes, it may be better to purchase a home that is already complete and ready for occupancy.

A large number of building projects in India seem to get delayed, sometimes for years. Perhaps, because developers start selling their buildings before getting necessary approvals, or perhaps due to a slow market where a developer may simply decide to delay the project for monetary reasons.

Those who had purchased under construction homes, in such buildings, may have already paid large sums of money to builders; they cannot get their money back and usually have no option to wait until their homes are ready.

Purchase contracts favor builders and no compensation is usually given for delayed projects, unless a person wants to take builders to court. This is not an easy task in India and can take several years even before a case is even heard. Then it can last even ten years or more if builders want to drag it through appeals etc.

If you are in the market to purchase a home, ready to move in homes are certainly worth considering. This may be a better option, than buying a home that is under construction.

Advantages of Buying Ready to Move in Homes

- As the new home is ready, no wait time is involved. Get possession as soon as you pay and complete paperwork.
- Most important, you know exactly what you are getting. You can see actual rooms, fixtures, facilities.
- No guess work as to how rooms will look. It is generally not easy to visualize a layout by just looking at sketches.

- Quite often what you see on home layout sketches and brochures, can be changed arbitrarily by the builder. Such changes are covered by builders in their sale/purchase documents, which people usually don't bother reading or fail to understand.

Sometimes people are given the impression that the price of a readymade home is higher than under construction homes. This is not always true and depends on market conditions. Most builders will accept reasonable offers in today's economy.

Negotiation on property that is ready and waiting for a buyer is always a good possibility. Every day the home lies vacant the builder is probably losing money.

Precautions when buying property in India

Whether you are buying a flat from a builder that is under construction, a property that is being re-sold or land in India, there are some precautions that purchasers should take. Lawyers, escrow companies etc. abroad, may have error & omissions covered through insurance. In India though, I doubt if such coverages are mandatory for lawyers. Do your research when hiring people to verify property sale/purchase documents.

Legal remedy for property disputes in India is very slow, expensive and time consuming. Some precautions and inquiries before purchasing property may help you avoid future problems.

Title Report – When purchasing property

A title report is basically a document meant to show how the builder obtained title to the land on which they are constructing homes to sell. Title report should be prepared by the seller and the purchaser's lawyer should check it to ensure that the title is clear and marketable.

Normally such reports are for a period of the last 30 years, showing ownership/ transfer details of the land. This helps to ascertain the present owner of the land. Buyers should get a detailed report, don't get satisfied by just a one page certificate.

Title report helps in determining that the land indeed is legally owned by the builder, and he is not constructing on land that is in dispute.

Purchasing Property under Construction

When buying a new property some of the things that require attention are:

- Ensure that the developer has clear title to the land, and that the relevant local authorities have approved the building plans.
- Check purchase agreements carefully, don't assume everything is standard and can't be taken out of a purchase agreement. Verbal agreements and assurances have no value. Get everything in writing. READ the purchase agreement, do this before paying a big deposit.
- If possible, don't buy a flat without parking space. India appears to have a new car out in the market every six months, but there is a severe shortage of parking. The value of your parking space will probably appreciate more than your flat!
- Get in writing the date of completion and remedy if the property is not completed in time.

Completion and occupation certificates are issued by the local government authorities after construction is complete and ready for occupancy.

This document is to indicate that the building has adhered to municipal requirements and is a very important document.

Clarify in writing in your purchase agreement that the builder will provide you with this certificate in a timely manner.

Renting Property in India

The property rental market in India continues to boom. Residential and commercial rental market in major cities across India has risen steadily and rental prices, are in many instances higher than what some pay in western countries. Some of the reasons for increased rental demand:

- Government policy changes towards foreign investment.
- International businesses locating to India.
- A booming Indian economy.
- India's population of 1.21 billion!
- Joint family system appears to be slowing down as the younger generation prefers to live independently.

Finding appropriate rental facilities is no easy task and most cities have property dealers who deal exclusively with rentals. NRIs who wish to invest in India, should keep the rental market in India in mind. Non-residents can rent their property in India and even have the rental income sent to them abroad.

Non-Residents renting out their property

NRIs, who own properties in India that, are currently vacant, may consider renting out their properties. Rents in the major cities have gone up in the last few years. It does make good economic sense, to rent out vacant properties. Some people shy away from renting, as they are worried about tenants who may not vacate the premises.

While there are no full proof methods, of protecting landlords in India from tenants, there are some steps landlords can take to protect themselves and their property. This can be done by not signing a normal rental lease agreement and using a leave and license agreement when renting out their property.

Types of rental agreements

There are normally two types of agreements that are used when renting property.

1. Rental Lease Agreement
2. Leave and license agreement

While both these types of agreements appear to be similar, for the purpose of renting property, there is a considerable difference when legal aspects are taken into consideration.

To clarify:

- In rental lease agreements, there is considered to be a transfer of interest from a lessor to a lessee.
- A Leave and License agreement does not create any interest in the premises in favor of the licensee.

NRIs and PIO who wish to rent out their properties should consider using a Leave and License agreement.

Leave and License agreements

License is defined in Section 52 of the Indian Easements Act, 1882. License simply gives the licensee the right to use and occupy the premises, for a limited duration, in consideration of the price paid.

When any property is given way of a license, the agreement is known as a 'leave and license agreement'. These agreements can be terminated according to the terms of the agreement and offer a higher form of protection to landlords, against tenants.

In case of eviction, generally rent control laws do not apply to leave and license agreements. Eviction under leave and license is governed by the Easements Act.

Where a license period has expired, immediate eviction of the tenant (license holder) may be sought. Tenants, occupying a property under a leave and license agreement can be evicted by the authorities when their license expires. Furthermore, from the date the license expires and until the day of eviction, the license fee (rent) payable to the landlord is automatically doubled*.

* This provision is under the Maharashtra Rent Control Act; please note that in other States of India, rent control laws may or may not apply, or apply differently to leave and license agreements executed in their State.

Drafting a Leave and License Agreement

When preparing a Leave and License agreement, it is of utmost importance that care is taken, to ensure that the document cannot be misinterpreted to be lease agreement.

Many Leave and License agreements have been challenged as being an agreement to lease and have ended up in courts. It is important to draft a leave and license agreement, so that it cannot be mistaken for an ordinary rental agreement.

It may be best for NRIs to hire a professional to draft such agreements. Ensure that the word 'license' is used instead of 'rent' or 'lease'.

Extract from:

Section 24 of Maharashtra Rent Control Act 1999

24. Landlord entitled to recover possession of premises given on license on expiry.

(1) Notwithstanding anything contained in this Act, a licensee in possession or occupation of premises given to him on license for residence shall deliver possession of such premises to the landlord on expiry of the period of license; and on the failure of the licensee to so deliver the possession of the licensed premises, a landlord shall be entitled to recover possession of such premises from a licensee, on the expiry of the period of license, by making an application to the Competent Authority, and, the Competent Authority, on being satisfied that the period of license has expired, shall pass an order for eviction of a licensee.

(2) Any licensee who does not deliver possession of the premises to the landlord on expiry of the period of license and continues to be in possession of the licensed premises till he is dispossessed by the Competent Authority shall be liable to pay damages at double the rate of the license fee or charge of the premises fixed under the agreement of license.

(3) The Competent Authority shall not entertain any claim of whatever nature from any other person who is not a licensee according to the agreement of license.

♦♦♦

Difference Lease Agreement - Leave & License

Leave & License	Lease / Rental Agreement
Possession is said to remain with the landlord, the licensee only gets permission to use the premises.	Possession in such cases passes to tenant.
Subletting is not possible under leave and license agreement.	Subletting may be possible under either the lease agreement or by rental legislation laws.
Rent control does not apply.	Rent controls may apply as per rent laws if any.
In a case where, the person who is the licensor of the property dies. The license is automatically terminated.	Lease agreement would not terminate in case of death of the landlord.
Advance rent can be charged.	Would be subject to provisions of the applicable Rent Control Legislation.
Easier eviction possible after expiry of license.	Regulated by Rent Control laws and may take more time if tenant contests.

Register Leave and License Agreement

A leave and license agreement must be duly registered. Unless registration is done, you will not be able to seek any relief from courts, in case a dispute arises. There is a small cost involved to register such documents in India. The amount required to be paid is calculated based on the rent, deposit and duration of the agreement.

My advice is to pay the required fee and get the registration done. In many cases the courts don't even want to hear a case if the agreement was not duly registered.

Tips when giving property on Leave and License

- Don't let out your property to anyone unless you check the person who is renting the property. While it is not possible in India to get background check done easily, you could take some precautions, such as checking the person's employment record, previous address etc.
- Don't hand over your property in trust and good faith to anyone regardless of how well they impress you, without checking proper documentation and finding out who exactly is going to occupy your property. When renting to a foreigner, local police should be informed. This is now required by law in many cities across India.
- Use a professional to draft the agreement. A lawyer is preferable than real estate brokers who have a pre written template for such agreements and just fill in the blanks.
- Pay the required stamp duty for your agreement and register it legally. Unless the agreement is registered, you

have no protection. The registration fee depends on the amount of license fee the landlord will be charging.

- If property is located in a society, then take a No Objection Certificate (NOC) from the society so as to avoid problems in future.
- It may be advisable to enter into an agreement of only eleven months and renew if you find things are working out well for you. However normally leave and license agreements allow one month notice to either parties to vacate the premises.
- In cases where a rental agent, such as a broker brings the client, you may consider adding in the agreement that no further brokerage will be paid, if and when the license agreement is renewed. Brokers in India normally charge one month rent as their fee.
- Do not let a high deposit for a rental influence your decision in selecting a tenant. Verify before accepting a tenant.
- Don't give possession of the property unless leave & license registration has been done.

♦♦♦

NRI Property – FAQ

Can NRIs rent out their property in India

An NRI can rent their property without RBI approval. The rental proceeds can be credited to their NRO account.

Repatriation of rental income

Rent proceeds deposited in NRO accounts can be freely repatriated. The Reserve Bank of India *(Circular No 45 dated. 14th May, 2002)* has clarified/instructed bankers to allow repatriation of current income like rent, dividend, pension, interest, etc.

Those NRIs who do not maintain an NRO account in India, repatriation can still be allowed based on an appropriate certification by a Chartered Accountant, certifying that the amount proposed to be remitted is eligible for remittance and that applicable taxes have been paid.

What is deemed rental income

As per the Indian Income Tax Act, if a person owns more than one residential property, only one of them will be deemed as self-occupied.

There is no income tax on a self-occupied property. The other one, whether you rent it out or not, will be deemed to have been given out on rent.

Even though the second property is not rented, the owner will have to calculate deemed rental income on the second property (based on certain valuations prescribed by the income tax rules) and pay the tax on deemed rental income accordingly.

Copy of RBI Notification Allowing Repatriation of Rental Income

Remittance of Current Income by NRIs.

A.P. (DIR Series) Circular No. 45 (May 14, 2002)

RESERVE BANK OF INDIA
EXCHANGE CONTROL DEPARTMENT
CENTRAL OFFICE MUMBAI - 400 001

A.P. (DIR Series) Circular No. 45

To
All Authorised Dealers in Foreign Exchange

May 14, 2002

Madam/Sirs,

Remittance of Current Income by NRIs.

As you are aware, authorised dealers can allow remittance of current income in India by debit to the Non-Resident (Ordinary) Rupee (NRO) accounts of the account holders vide paragraph 3(B)(ii) of Schedule 3 to Notification No. FEMA.5/ 2000-RB dated May 3, 2000 issued under the Foreign Exchange Management Act, 1999.

2. Authorised Dealers may, henceforth, allow repatriation of current income like rent, dividend, pension, interest, etc. of NRIs who do not maintain an NRO account in India based on an appropriate certification by a Chartered Accountant, certifying that the amount proposed to be remitted is eligible for remittance and that applicable taxes have been paid/provided for.

3. Authorised Dealers may bring the contents of the circular to the notice of their constituents concerned.

4. The directions contained in this circular have been issued under Section 10(4) and Section 11(1) of the Foreign Exchange Management Act, 1999 (42 of 1999).

Yours faithfully,
Grace Koshie

Chief General

Is rental income taxed in India?

Rental income from properties located in India is taxable in India. Tax will normally be deducted at source by the payer of the rent. Any person, who deducts or collects tax at source on behalf of the Income tax department, is required to apply for and obtain [Tax Deduction and Collection Account Number (TAN) from the tax department.

Normally the tenant should:

1. Obtain a TAN.
2. Deduct 30% as TDS from the rental payment.
3. Give a receipt of the deduction to the landlord by issuing a TDS receipt.
4. Submit the tax withheld to the tax department.

In case the tenant does not deduct tax and the NRI fails to declare the income and pay the tax due, the income tax authorities may hold the person paying the rent responsible. In case the tenant does not deduct tax from the rental payments. NRI landlords should consider filing a tax return in India to declare the rental income.

Incase their tenant has deducted TDS on rent, then depending on the applicable tax slab in India, the landlord can claim a tax refund, that they may be entitled to by filling a tax return.

Rental income taxed in the country of residence

Most countries tax residents on their global income. Hence there is a possibility that NRIs may be liable to pay tax, on their rental income in India, as well as their country of residence. However, in such cases, the Double Taxation Avoidance

Agreements that India has entered into with various countries, should provide NRIs some relief.

For example, the tax treaty (DTAA) between India and the United States of America for instance provides that rent from immovable property will be taxed in the country in which the property is situated.

NRIs who are residents of USA and have properties rented out in India are required to pay tax on the rental income in India. When they file their US taxes they would declare their foreign rental income and claim a credit for the tax paid in India.

Capital gains taxation on property

Profits arising out of sale of property are taxable as capital gains in the year in which the sale takes place.

As per the Income Tax Act, 1961, capital gain can be either short term, or a long term capital gain. Different rates of tax apply for gains on transfer of long term and short-term capital assets.

Capital gains on property can be saved from taxation if the gains are long term and invested again in India as per applicable rules and guidelines.

Short term capital gain

When assets sold were held for less than 36 months, the gain is considered to be a short term capital gain. In case of shares, debentures and mutual fund units, the period of holding required is only 12 months.

Gains on short-term capital assets are taxed as regular income.

Long term capital gain

When assets are sold after being held for more than 36 months, it is considered to be a long term capital gain. Long term capital gain on property that has been held for over 36 months is taxed @ 20%.

Exemption from Capital Gains

In some cases, Hindu undivided family (HUF) or individuals may be exempt from long term capital gains. Long-term capital gain arising from sale of property is exempt under Section 54/54F, if the money from the proceeds of the sale is reinvested in certain assets such as, in the purchase of a new house or long term bonds such as:

- NHAI [National Highway Authority of India]
- REC [Rural Electrification Corporation Ltd]

If investment is made in a property to avail benefits of capital gains exemption, then from the assessment year 22015-2016, such investment must be in a residential house situated in India and not abroad.

Undervaluing sale price of property to save taxes

Trying to reduce capital gains by accepting payments in the form of cash, to cheat the system is not advised. Property brokers in India may give non-residents the impression that such real-estate transactions are common in India. They may be common, but are illegal. Things have changed in India now and property registrars are more vigilant and fully aware of such schemes.

Circle Rates for property sale/purchase

When a property is purchased or sold in India, generally the purchaser pays the cost of the stamp duty involved to get the property registration formalities completed.

The cost of the stamp duty is based on the sale price of the property being registered. The seller of the property would be liable to pay capital gains depending on his purchase and selling price.

Since both seller and buyer become liable to pay tax (stamp duty/capital gain) based on the price of the property there is a tendency to register the property for an amount lower than the actual consideration being paid. The seller may accept cash of an agreed upon amount and show the property being sold at a lower price.

To ensure that people do not cheat on their tax liability that occurs on sale of property, local governments have set minimum rates for property registration, these rates are called circle rates.

A circle rate is the minimum rate of valuation of land; houses, apartments etc. located in a particular colony *(neighborhood)*. Each colony would have a different circle rate based on valuation criteria used by the authorities.

No registration or sale of property can be done for an amount lower than the circle rate of the area where the property is located. Even if the sale/purchase agreement shows a lower amount, the registrar will levy stamp duty taking the circle rate into account.

For instance, Delhi has eight categories of colonies, A to H. The circle rate applicable to a property would be the colony rate in which the property is located.

To give readers an idea, the circle rates for the year 2015 applicable in Delhi area are shown in the table below.

Circle Rates per square meter for Delhi, India as of Sept, 23, 2014	
Category 'A' Colonies	Rs. 7.74 lakh
Category 'B' Colonies	Rs. 2.45 lakh
Category 'C' Colonies	Rs. 1.60 lakh
Category 'D' Colonies	Rs. 1.28 lakh
Category 'E' Colonies	Rs. 70,080
Category 'F' Colonies	Rs. 56,640
Category 'G' Colonies	Rs. 46,200
Category 'H' Colonies	Rs. 23,280

No registration or sale of property can be done for an amount less than the circle rate of the area where the property is located. Even if the sale/purchase agreement shows a lower amount, the registrar will levy stamp duty taking the circle rate into account.

♦ ♦ ♦

Calculating capital gains on sale of property

When it comes to capital gains on real-estate, some people believe that the selling price, minus the purchase price is their profit, and the amount on which they would be subjected to capital gains tax. For example:

Suppose you bought a house in India for Rupees 35 lakh in November 1995 and you sell this property in October 2010 for a price of say Rupees105 lakhs. Some people may assume that the capital gain on the sale of this property would be the selling price - purchase price which works out to a 70 lakhs.

Actually the calculation above is not correct. While deducting the purchase price of 35 Lakh, from the sale price of 105 Lakhs, gives you a profit of 70 Lakh, this is not your capital gain.

This is because when you factor in the cost inflation indexation, your taxable capital gain liability is reduced considerably.

Cost Inflation Indexing

One acceptable fact about money these days is that the value of the money decreases every year due to inflation.

The department of income tax in India allows indexing the cost price, so as to arrive at a price that is comparable to the sale price, when you sell your property.

This price is referred to as the **Indexed Cost of Acquisition**. More information on this topic and how to calculate capital gains is provided on the following pages.

♦♦♦

How to calculate Long term capital gains

The cost of acquisition of property that was purchased many years ago can be indexed, using the cost inflation index numbers. Cost inflation index is a number derived for each financial year by the Reserve Bank of India. This is done by taking into account the prevailing prices during that financial year.

Hence, if we see a change in the cost inflation index between the year 1995 and 2010, it would give us an indication of the change in prices between these years.

To start off, first you need to find the Indexation factor from the cost indexing inflation table. A sample of this table is provided.

Cost Inflation Index Chart

FINANCIAL YEAR	COST INFLATION INDEX
1981-1982	100
1982-1983	109
1983-1984	116
1984-1985	125
1985-1986	133
1986-1987	140
1987-1988	150

1988-1989	161
1989-1990	172
1990-1991	182
1991-1992	199
1992-1993	223
1993-1994	244
1994-1995	259
1995-1996	281
1996-1997	305
1997-1998	331
1998-1999	351
1999-2000	389
2000-2001	406
2001-2002	426
2002-2003	447
2003-2004	463

2004-2005	480
2005-2006	497
2006-2007	519
2007-2008	551
2008-2009	582
2009-2010	632
2010-2011	711
2011-2012	785
2012-2013	852
2013-2014	939
2014-2015	1024
2015-2016	1081

Formula to find the indexation factor:

Indexation Factor = Cost inflation index of the year of sale / Cost inflation index of the year of purchase.

Example: Suppose you purchased a house in November 1995 for Rupees 35 lakhs and decide to sell it for Rupees 105 lakhs in

October 2010. When you subtract the purchase price 35 lakh from the sale price of 105 lakh the gain appears to be 70 lakh. However this is not the amount on which capital gain tax needs to be paid as indexing has not been factored in.

Step by step example to calculate capital gain

Let's calculate the capital gains on such a transaction by applying the cost inflation index.

1. First we need to find the cost inflation index for the year of the sale. Using the cost inflation index chart table provided, we can see that the cost inflation index for the year 2010 when you want to sell is 711
2. The cost inflation index for the year 1995, when you purchased the property is 281.

So using the formula, Indexation Factor = Cost inflation index of the year of sale / Cost inflation index of the year of purchase: Indexation Factor = 711 / 281 = 2.53024

This means that the prices have increased around 2.5 times between the years 1995 and 2010.

To clarify further, what you bought for 35 lakhs in 1995 would cost 2.5 times more in 2010 due to inflation reducing the value of money.

Once you have calculated the indexation factor, you can calculate the indexed cost of your acquisition. This is done by multiplying the actual sale price by the indexation factor.

Formula: Indexed Cost of Acquisition = Actual Purchase Price * multiplied by the Indexation Factor.

So your Indexed cost of acquisition when applying this formula works out to 35 lakh * 2.53024 = 88.56 lakh. The actual capital gains that would apply for your property sale, can now be calculated.

Calculating your long term capital gain

Long term capital gain is the difference between the sale price and the indexed cost of your acquisition.

Formula: Long Term Capital Gain = Sale Price - Indexed Cost of Acquisition.

Using the amounts from our example:

Long Term Capital Gain = Rs. 105 Lakh – Rs. 88.56 Lakh. This works out to Rs. 16.44 Lakh.

So the capital gain that seemed to be Rs. 70 lakh is actually only Rupees 16.44 lakhs. This can even be further reduced, when you add all the expenses for your property upgrades, maintenance etc. and apply indexing to those figures also.

Suppose Rupees 6.44 lakh was spent in making improvements to the property after you bought it in 1995. Then your final figure is trimmed down to a capital gain of 10 lakh. Considering a 20% capital gains tax rate, you would have to pay just 2 lakhs.

Cost inflation index for prior years:

The benefit of indexation can be availed, either from the year of acquisition of the property by the assesse, or from the base year 1981-82, whichever is later. The financial year in India is from April to March. When reading the cost inflation index chart, the month of purchase needs to be taken into consideration.

Repatriate money from sale of property

NRIs/PIO, who sell real estate they own in India, and wish to transfer money from the sale proceeds of their property abroad. Quite often use private money transfer methods to remit money abroad. Private money transfer, known as 'Hawala' is an illegal method of remittance, there is also a risk that you may not get your money.

There was a time when money, could not be transferred abroad from India without going through a lot of red tape. However things have now changed for the better. Money that is legally owned and accounted for, can quite easily be remitted abroad through normal banking channels, in a safe and legal manner.

Legal method to repatriate money from India

The Reserve Bank of India has delegated powers, to authorized dealers of foreign exchange to process applications and effect repatriation.

There are certain guidelines that need to be followed, when it comes to transferring money that is received from the sale of property abroad.

In case the property was purchased, with money received from inward remittance or debit to NRE/FCNR/NRO account, then the principal amount can be repatriated outside India.

Example: *250,000 US$ are sent from abroad by an NRI to purchase property in India. Suppose the property is sold for a sum that is equivalent to US$350,000.The principal amount of*

US$ 250,000, can be repatriated immediately. The balance would be deposited in an NRO account.

Prior to June 2002 there was a lock in period for sale of property proceeds to be repatriated by NRIs. Non-Resident Indians & Persons of Indian origin could repatriate sale proceeds of immovable property provided the sale took place after three years from the date of acquisition of such property. The lock in period was removed effective November 1, 2002.

Excerpt from RBI notification

Reserve Bank has issued Notification No. FEMA 65/2002-RB dated June 29, 2002 (copy enclosed) amending the Notification cited above, removing the existing lock-in period for repatriation of the sale proceeds of immovable property purchased in India by NRIs/PIO.

Accordingly, it will be in order for authorised dealers to allow remittance of sale proceeds of immovable property in India acquired by NRIs/PIO, irrespective of the period for which the property was held. The sale proceeds allowed to be repatriated should, however, not exceed the foreign exchange brought in to acquire the property.

In case the property was purchased out of Rupee resources, then the money from the sale of property can be credited to the NRO account of the NRI/PIO.

NRIs are allowed to repatriate an amount up to USD one million, per financial year, from their NRO account. Such transfers are allowed, subject to tax compliance. The limit of US dollars 1 million includes sale proceeds of up to two immovable properties held by NRIs/PIO.

How to repatriate money from sale of property

To be able to transfer money, received in India from the sale of your property, it is important that the payment for the property is accepted through legal banking channels.

Documentary proof showing source of money will be required when transferring money abroad. In order to transfer the money it must first be deposited in an NRO bank account.

Step by step guide to transfer money abroad

1. To start the repatriation process, the first step is to get a certificate from a Chartered Accountant (CA) in India.

CA Certificate Information

The certificate required from a chartered account, is actually issued on a form that is called 'Form 15CB'. This form can be downloaded by simply logging on to the Indian government tax website, and downloading it.

The website page to access the form is: https://www.tin-nsdl.com/download/Form15CB.pdf

The CA will fill in the form and sign it. Basically the form is to verify that the money being sent abroad, has indeed been acquired from legal sources such as, from the sale of your property and all taxes that were due have been paid. The CA will verify and sign the Form for you.

2. Once you have the completed CA certificate on 'Form 15CB' the next step involves filling a Form called Form 15CA.

What is Form 15CA?

This is a form that is filed online with the tax department. Prior to Feb, 2014 this form was easily accessible from the income tax website, could be filled and submitted online. However, now to access FORM 15CA you would have to go to the Indian tax department website: https://incometaxindiaefiling.gov.in/ and unless you have already registered with the tax department, you will be required to complete their registration process. This is required before you can access any Forms on their website.

To register you need a PAN Number. If you don't have one, getting it is pretty easy and explained in the Pan Card article of this book.

3. Once you are registered and able to login
4. Go to the E-file option
5. Select appropriate option to prepare & submit forms online other than your income tax return (ITR)
6. Selecting this option shows various forms. Select FORM 15CA from the list.
7. Select Part A or Part B depending on the type of remittances you are doing.
8. Fill form with all required fields and submit.
9. After successful submission a transaction ID and acknowledgement number appears and should be printed. This will be required as proof of submission by the bank when you wish to transfer funds.
    - Verification can also be done after submission.
    - Go to My account-My Returns/Forms. It will show all the returns and the Forms submitted.

- Click on the 15CA form and take a printout of Form along with acknowledgement Slip.

10. The final step, involves taking the signed undertaking along with the CA certificate on Form 15CB, to the bank where you have your NRO account. Your bank will transfer your money abroad. No further permission is required by banks as RBI has authorized dealers to submit funds once the above mentioned documents are provided.

Requirement to file Form 15 CA/CB – update

The requirement to file information on Forms 15CA/15CB comes under Rule 37BB. Due to revisions to Rule 37BB the following changes came into effect from October 1, 2013:

- If the amount being submitted does not exceed fifty thousand rupees and the aggregate of such payments made during the financial year does not exceed two lakh fifty thousand rupees then remitter must fill in the information required in Part A of Form No.15CA
- Fill in the information in Part B of Form No.15CA if the funds being remitted are not chargeable to tax and is of the nature specified in the **transfer of funds purpose list** shown below:

Acceptable purpose list - 'Transfer of Funds Abroad'

1. Indian investment abroad -in equity capital (shares)
2. Indian investment abroad -in debt securities
3. Indian investment abroad -in branches and wholly owned subsidiaries

4. Indian investment abroad -in subsidiaries and associates
5. Indian investment abroad -in real estate
6. Postal services
7. Construction of projects abroad by Indian companies including import of goods at project site
8. Freight insurance - relating to import and export of goods
9. Payments for maintenance of offices abroad
10. Maintenance of Indian embassies abroad
11. Loans extended to Non-Residents
12. Remittances by foreign embassies in India
13. Payment for operating expenses of Indian shipping companies operating abroad.
14. Remittance by non-residents towards family maintenance and savings
15. Operating expenses of Indian Airlines companies operating abroad
16. Remittance towards personal gifts and donations
17. Booking of passages abroad - Airlines companies
18. Remittance towards donations to religious and charitable institutions abroad
19. Remittance towards business travel
20. Remittance towards grants and donations to other governments and charitable institutions established by the governments
21. Travel under basic travel quota (BTQ)
22. Contributions or donations by the Government to international institutions
23. Travel for pilgrimage

24. Remittance towards payment or refund of taxes
25. Travel for medical treatment
26. Refunds or rebates or reduction in invoice value on account of exports
27. Travel for education (including fees, hostel expenses etc.)
28. Payments by residents for international bidding

Documents bank will require

- Form 15CA.
- Form 15CB in duplicate signed by the Chartered Accountant
- Form A2 – Your bank should supply you with this form, a sample form A2 is included in this book.
- Application for foreign exchange- this form would also be supplied by the bank

Banks may want some additional documentation depending on the source of the money being remitted. In case the source of the money being transferred abroad, is from the sale of property in India. To verify that the person who is sending the money abroad, did have legal ownership of the property and the transmission of funds are indeed the sale proceeds of that property; banks may want to see proof such as:

- Copy of the sale document of the property.
- If the property had been inherited then copy of the WILL, legal heir certificate, death certificate on whose death the property has been inherited.

While CA certificate should suffice, each bank may have their own set of rules. My perception is that while the government of India is trying to help non-residents, by easing restrictions and giving authority to banks to remit funds, on being provided with CA certification in the authorized format. Some banks go out of their way to create hurdles by asking for documents, that perhaps are not even required and cause an extra burden on NRIs who are in India for short visits.

If you have problems with a bank, perhaps it's time to share your experience with other NRIs and look for a more customer friendly bank.

Plan repatriation of funds

While the repatriation procedure is fairly simple, with some planning you can probably make it much easier.

- It might be prudent, for non-residents, to consult a CA **before** selling their property in India. They can guide you how to accept money from the sale proceeds and what documentation to get.
- CA can help in calculating as well as methodically paying any taxes that may be due, on the sale of your property. Remember, your CA has to verify that taxes have been paid on 'Form 15CB'.

Ten year lock in if property purchased in Indian currency

In case of property that was bought with funds generated from Indian sources is sold, then the sale proceeds can be repatriated only if:

1. The property is being sold after being held for a period

of ten years.

2. If the property is sold before the ten years period, then the sale proceeds must be deposited in a NRO account until the ten year period is completed. See example below for clarification.

Example:

Property sold after being held for eight years, in such a case the sale proceeds must be deposited in NRO account for two years to complete the 10 year required for repatriation.

Note: The waiting period of 10 years for repatriation of sale proceeds of property sold in India will not apply if property sold was purchased by NRIs in foreign exchange funds. Proof that money was sent for the purchase from abroad may be required.

♦♦♦

Buying Agricultural land

Purchasing agricultural land in India is restricted in many States of India, not only for NRIs, but also for Indian citizens.

Each state has its own policy when it comes to purchase of agricultural land in their state. For example, in the state of Maharashtra, Gujarat and Karnataka, only Indian residents who are agriculturists can purchase agricultural land. There seem to be no such restrictions in the state of Tamil Nadu.

Non-resident Indians, Persons of Indian origin and OCI holders are not allowed to buy agricultural land anywhere in India.

To clarify, while Indian citizens, who may not have a farming background, may be allowed to buy agricultural land in some Indian States. NRIs, PIO or OCI holders cannot do so.

Conversion of Agricultural Land

Generally agricultural land is classified in two categories:

1. Wet Land [land suitable for cultivation]
2. Dry Land

State Governments in India may allow the conversion of Dry Land that is not suitable for cultivation. Each State may have their own set of rules and procedures for conversion. Tamil Nadu for example, allows Dry agricultural land to be converted to non-agricultural land if no agricultural activity has taken place on the land for a period of ten years.

Generally conversion of agricultural land is not an easy matter. Anyone thinking of buying agricultural land for non-agricultural purposes, should do their research prior to purchase.

How NRIs can acquiring agricultural land in India

NRIs are NOT allowed to purchase agricultural land, anywhere in India. This applies to all states of India. The only way NRIs can acquire agricultural land, is by way of inheritance. NRIs cannot be gifted agricultural land. Quite often I get emails sent to my website FAQ section from NRIs/PIO intent on buying agricultural land in India. I get the impression that these NRIs assume that agricultural land is cheaper or they wish to purchase land for other business projects.

The reality is that agricultural land in India is certainly not cheap these days. The only way a huge profit can be made is getting agricultural land converted to non-agricultural and this is not easily done.

Generally, some people in India may want to acquire agricultural land not because they are keen on farming, but for tax benefits. Income that is considered to be from agricultural projects is tax free in India and owning agricultural land seems to be the route to lower taxation.

All said and done, NRIs/PIO cannot legally purchase or acquire agricultural land in India by way of a gift. The only way NRIs can acquire agricultural land, is by way of inheritance.

Foreigners acquiring Agricultural Land in India

Foreign nationals of non-Indian origin can acquire agricultural land in India, by way of inheritance. They cannot purchase or be gifted agricultural land. However, a citizen of Pakistan, Bangladesh, Sri Lanka, Afghanistan, China, Iran, Nepal and

Bhutan, should seek prior approval of the Reserve Bank for inheriting any type of immovable property in India.

Sale scams involving agricultural land

Non-resident Indians, should be aware of current rules and regulations before trying to purchase agricultural land in India. Ignorance of the law is never accepted as a reason for breaking the law.

Some agents may try and sell off agricultural property, with verbal guarantees that they will handle all the paper work and registration.

Guarantees and promises made by property brokers may however turn out to be worthless. If registration of land is done based on incorrect information about the purchaser, the validity of the registration would be questionable.

In cases where a person's non-resident status is purposely hidden, for the purpose of acquiring agricultural land, they may face not only the loss of the property but also legal penalties. Furthermore, non-residents need to act within the framework of the laws of India, or risk losing their Indian visas.

Agricultural land use for new business venture

Those who require land in India for a new business venture, may be tempted to consider agricultural land as an option, not only due to the high prices of land in urban areas, but also the availability issue.

However conversion of agricultural land to allow commercial use is not a simple task.

Those non-residents, who wish to purchase land for business purposes, may stand a better chance of approaching the relevant government authority where the land is located to check if conversion is possible and guidelines on getting land converted.

Conversion of land where it is beneficial to the local government stands a fair chance of approval.

Agricultural land owned before becoming NRI

There is no law that forces Indian citizens who currently own agricultural land, to sell their agricultural land if they become non-residents or acquire foreign citizenship.

NRIs who legally owned agricultural land, before becoming non-residents can continue to own, their agricultural land in India.

NRIs gifting agricultural land they own in India

NRI/PIO, who own agricultural land/plantation property or farm house in India, can gift such properties, only to a person resident in India, who is a citizen of India. They cannot gift to another non-resident Indian, or to a foreigner.

A foreign national of non-Indian origin, must get prior approval from the Reserve Bank, to gift agricultural land or plantation property/farm house in India.

Any property that is acquired in India, by not following the currency exchange requirements that were applicable when the property was acquired, cannot be gifted or passed on by way of inheritance.

Sale of agricultural land owned by NRI/PIO

Some NRIs may own agricultural land in India that had been acquired, before they became non-residents. If they wish to sell their agricultural lands, they can sell them only to a citizen of India, who is a resident in India. They cannot sell to another NRI.

No payment for any type of property that is located in India can be made abroad. This applies, even if the person to whom you are selling, is an Indian citizen resident in India.

♦ ♦ ♦

Sale of agricultural land owned by foreigners

There is a possibility that a foreign national on non-Indian origin, may own agricultural land in India. They may have got ownership by way of inheritance. In such cases, if a foreign national of non-Indian origin, who resides outside India decides to sell their agricultural land, they would need **prior approval** of the Reserve Bank of India to sell.

As per RBI guidelines, foreign nationals, who acquire immoveable property, by way of inheritance in India, are required to get RBI permission, before they can transfer ownership of such property.

Sending foreign currency out of India

Rules applicable to sending money out of India have been relaxed considerably over the last few years. India no longer lacks foreign exchange. The government of India has simplified and liberalized foreign exchange facilities available to Indian residents. Indian citizens can now, without any permission from the RBI purchase and transfer foreign exchange through authorized foreign exchange dealers.

Small value remittances of foreign exchange

The Reserve Bank of India (RBI) allows residents to remit up to USD 5000/- on current account towards various small value transactions such as, payment for services, subscriptions, and purchases, with minimum formalities. This foreign exchange remittance scheme is not allowed for prohibited purchases such as lottery tickets etc.

RBI has given permission to authorized dealers to release foreign exchange not exceeding USD 5,000 or its equivalent for all permissible current account transactions. Authorized dealers such as your bank, may obtain simplified Application-cum-Declaration form (Form A2) from the remitter.

For remittances up to US$ 500, normally the only document required to be produced is a simple letter from the applicant containing the basic information such as, name and address of the applicant, name and address of the beneficiary to whom the money is to be sent and the purpose of remittance. For amounts over US$500, your bank will provide you with Form A2.

Sample Form A2

Form A2
Application cum Declaration
(To be completed by the applicant)

Application for drawal of foreign exchange
I. Details of the applicant -
a. Name: ____________________________
b. Address: ____________________________________
c. Account No. : _____________________
II. Details of the foreign exchange required
1. Amount (Specify currency) : ___________________
2. Purpose: __________________________________
III. I authorize you to debit my Saving Bank/Current/RFC/EEFC Account No.________________ together with your charges and
* a) Issue a draft : Beneficiary's Name __________________
Address ________________________________
* b) Effect the foreign exchange remittance directly -
1. Beneficiary's Name: ___________________________
2. Name and address of the Bank: _________________
3. Account No. : ____________________
* c) Issue travelers cheques for _______________________
* d) Issue foreign currency notes for ___________________
⍰ (Strike out whichever is not applicable)

Signature

Declaration(Under FEMA 1999)I,________________________ declare that

* 1) The total amount of foreign exchange purchased from or remitted through, all sources in India during this calendar year including this application is within USD _____________ (USD _____________ only) the annual limit prescribed by Reserve Bank of India for the said purpose.
* 2) Foreign exchange purchased from you is for the purpose indicated above.
⍰ (Strike out whichever is not applicable)
Signature
Name Date:

Liberalized Remittances Scheme of USD 250,000

This scheme is applicable to all Indian resident individuals, including minors and permits them to make remittances of up to US$ 250,000 per financial year (April – March) for any permissible current or capital account transaction or a combination of both.

A PAN card is mandatory to make a remittance under this scheme. In case of remitter being a minor, the LRS declaration form must be countersigned by the minor's natural guardian.

Allowed under Liberalized Remittances Scheme

Under the Scheme, the foreign exchange sent abroad can be used to acquire and hold without the prior approval of the Reserve Bank of India:

- Immovable property
- shares
- debt instruments
- Or any other assets outside India.

Individuals can also open, maintain and hold foreign currency accounts with banks outside India, for carrying out transactions permitted under the Scheme. *(More info: www.rbi.org.in)*

There are also some restrictions for which this scheme cannot be used to send money abroad.

See prohibited items listed on the next page.

♦♦♦

Restrictions prohibited items under LRS Scheme

The liberalized remittance scheme does impose some restrictions, on sending money out for purposes such as:

- Remittance for any purpose specifically prohibited under *Schedule 1 *(list provided on next page)*
- Any item restricted under Schedule II of Foreign Exchange Management (Current Account Transactions) Rules, 2000.
- Remittance from India for margins or margin calls to overseas exchanges/overseas counterparty.
- Remittances for purchase of FCCB issued by Indian companies in the overseas secondary market.
- Remittance for trading in foreign exchange abroad.
- Remittance by a resident individual for setting up a company abroad.
- Remittances directly or indirectly to Bhutan, Nepal, Mauritius and Pakistan.
- Remittances directly or indirectly to those individuals and entities identified as posing significant risk of committing acts of terrorism as advised separately by the Reserve Bank to the banks.
- Remittances directly or indirectly to countries identified by the *Financial Action Task Force (FATF) as 'non co-operative countries and territories' from time to time;

  *The Financial Action Task Force (FATF) is an inter-governmental body to combat money laundering and terrorist financing. For more information on FATF, visit http://www.fatf-gafi.org/

The facility under the 'Liberalized Remittance Scheme' is in addition to foreign exchange that is allowed for private travel, business travel, studies, medical treatment, etc.

*Schedule I

indi

- Remittance out of lottery winnings.
- Remittance of income from racing/riding etc. or any other hobby.
- Remittance for purchase of lottery tickets, banned/proscribed magazines, football pools, sweepstakes, etc.
- Payment of commission on exports made towards equity investment in Joint Ventures/ Wholly Owned Subsidiaries abroad of Indian companies.
- Remittance of dividend by any company to which the requirement of dividend balancing is applicable.
- Payment of commission on exports under Rupee State Credit Route, except commission up to 10% of invoice value of exports of tea and tobacco.
- Payment related to 'Call Back Services' of telephones.

*Foreign Exchange Management (Current Account Transactions) Rules, 2000 Notification No. G.S.R.381 (E) dated 3rd May.

♦ ♦ ♦

NRI Paying foreign loans from India

Non-resident Indians who prior to their return to India, had taken a loan abroad, for which they still need to make payments, can use the liberalized remittance scheme to make such loan payments.

Send money using the Liberalized Remittance Scheme

The person remitting money using this scheme should have a bank account with an authorized bank for at least one year as per RBI guidelines. Your bank is obligated to confirm to their satisfaction that:

1. The funds belong to you.
2. The purpose of the remittance, so as to ensure that the funds will not be used for the purposes prohibited or regulated under the Scheme.

Frequency of sending money

There is no restriction on the frequency. The only requirement is that the total amount of foreign exchange purchased from or remitted, through all sources in India during a financial year, should be within the cumulative limit of US$ 250,000.

Remittance of current income

Remittance of current income such as rent, dividend, pension, interest etc. of NRIs/PIO is repatriable on the basis of appropriate certification by a Chartered Accountant certifying, that the amount proposed to be remitted, is eligible for remittance and that applicable taxes, have been paid or acceptable arrangements have been made to pay the taxes.

NRIs/PIO have the option to credit the current income to their Non-Resident (External) Rupee account, provided the bank is satisfied that the credit represents current income of the non-resident account holder and any applicable income tax has been deducted or acceptable arrangements made to pay the taxes.

Remittance of assets from India by a foreigner

An amount of up to one million US$ can be transferred by a foreign national of non-Indian origin who has:

- Retired from employment in India or
- Who has inherited assets from a person resident in India or
- Who is a widow of an Indian citizen who was resident in India

The person sending the money abroad would be required to submit proof by way of documentary evidence of the source of the money being sent abroad. For instance, if the source of the funds is by way of inheritance, then proof such as copy of a Will.

They would also have to provide the bank through which the transaction is being conducted, a certificate from a Chartered Accountant. The CA certificate should be in the formats prescribed by the Central Board of Direct Taxes, as per circular NO.10/2002 dated October 9, 2002.

The CA certificate is normally to verify that all taxes, applicable to the money being sent out, have been paid or arrangements have been made to ensure that the taxes will be paid.

These remittance facilities are not available to citizens of Nepal and Bhutan.

Remit funds abroad from NRO Account

NRIs/PIO may transfer out of India an amount up to one million US dollars per financial year, out of the balances held in their Non-Resident Ordinary (NRO) Rupee account, subject to submitting required documents in the prescribed format as evidence that provides proof of the source of the funds being repatriated and that any taxes, if due have been paid.

Types of Assets that can be sent abroad from NRO accounts

- Remittance is allowed for sale proceeds of assets such as immovable property
- Financial assets [such as shares/mutual funds]
- Assets acquired by way of inheritance
- Current income [such as rent, dividend, pension, interest income in India]

(Central Board of Direct Taxes vide their Circular NO.10/2002 dated October 9, 2002.)

Who is an authorized dealer of foreign exchange

The term authorized dealer, normally refers to banks and money agents in India who have been authorized by the Reserve Bank of India to deal in foreign exchange.

Authorized dealers, have been given authority by the Reserve Bank of India (RBI) to allow certain foreign exchange transactions, in line with applicable rules and regulations, without customers having to approach the RBI for permission.

A list of authorized dealers is available on the RBI website at http://www.fedai.org.in/

Sending money abroad from NRE account

NRE account balances are freely repatriable. Such a transaction can simply be done by either visiting your bank or even via online banking facility provided by some banks.

Deposit Current Income in India to NRE Account

NRE account holders who have current income in India such as rent, dividend, pension, bank interest income do have the option to get this type of income deposited in their NRE accounts instead of NRO account.

Since no tax applies to NRE accounts, no TDS is deducted from NRE accounts. Hence it is beneficial to have your money in NRE account. To have current income deposited in NRE account a request has to be made to your bank and some documentation has to be completed.

Repatriation of inherited assets

To transfer abroad, money received as inheritance or by selling inherited assets, non-residents are required to provide their bank, documentary evidence verifying their inherited assets.

They can then have the funds transferred abroad by providing an undertaking and a certificate by Chartered Accountant, in the prescribed format to the bank from where the money is to be transferred.

This remittance facility is not available to citizens of Pakistan, Bangladesh, Sri Lanka, China, Afghanistan, Iran, Nepal & Bhutan.

Banking in India

The operations of all banks in India come under the control of the Reserve Bank of India (RBI). India has two main categories of banks.

1. Public Sector Banks
2. Private Sector Banks

Public Sector Banks

Public sector banks are controlled and managed by the Government of India. Some of the well-known names of public sector banks are:

- State Bank of India
- Canara Bank
- Punjab National Bank
- Central Bank of India
- Vijaya Bank
- Syndicate Bank
- Allahabad Bank
- Andhra Bank
- Dena Bank
- Bank of India
- Corporation Bank
- Bank of Baroda

Private Sector Banks

Private sector banks are those where the majority stake is held by private shareholders and not by the government. Some of the well-known private sector banks are:

- Axis Bank
- Federal Bank
- HDFC Bank
- City Union Bank
- Catholic Syrian Bank
- ICICI Bank
- Kotak Bank
- Karnataka Bank
- Centurion Bank
- Bank of Punjab

Private sector banks started in India less than 20 years ago and when you consider that Allahabad Bank a public sector bank was founded in the year 1865, we can say that private banks are relatively new in India.

I would assume that the majority of NRIs hold their non-resident bank accounts in private sector banks, as they have an aggressive advertising campaign targeting NRIs across the globe. When Private Sector Banks started operations in India they started using computerized systems.

Private Sector Banks are also credited with having introduced online banking in India. Public Sector Banks such as the State Bank of India however, are still considered by many as safe banks as they are backed by the Government of India.

Type of Bank Accounts for NRIs

Predominantly there are three bank account options available for NRIs. Some of the salient features of each type of NRI bank account is given below:

Non Resident Ordinary Bank Account (NRO)

Salient features of NRO account

- Funds are held in Indian Rupees
- Interest earned on this account is taxable. TDS is deducted on this type of account. Currently TDS deduction is 30.9%
- Generally repatriation of funds not allowed, except for certain types of deposits for which repatriation is possible subject to providing required documents verifying source of funds and that taxes have been paid on the amount being remitted

- NRI/PIO account holder can have joint Indian individual as a joint account owner.

Non Resident External Bank Account (NRE)

Salient features of NRO account

- Transfer Funds freely between India and abroad
- Funds are held in Indian Rupees but converted to foreign currency when sent abroad.
- Interest earned on this type of account is not taxable in India. Hence no TDS deduction on NRE bank accounts.
- All funds in this type of account, including accrued interest can be freely repatriated without any type of permission or additional documentation
- Joint account allowed with a non-resident on 'former or survivor basis.
    - Account holder has the option to mandate someone to operate the account on his/her behalf. Power of Attorney may be required by bank
- Account holder can also avail the facility of getting an international debit card that can be used worldwide.
- Online banking, payment of local bills etc. may be provided by some banks to their NRE account holders

Foreign Currency Non Resident account (FCNR)

Salient features of FCNR account

- While NRE deposits are held in Indian currency, funds in FCNR account are held in foreign currency. Account holder can select any of the following currencies: US Dollars, Pounds Sterling, Euro, Japanese Yen, Australian Dollars or Canadian Dollars

- FCNR accounts are NOT normal bank accounts but fixed deposits, commonly known as term deposits abroad. Minimum deposit term is one year and account holders can opt for a maximum term of up to five years.
- Principle and Interest can be fully repatriated
- Can be opened jointly with other Non-residents

Understanding the various account types available might help NRIs in making an informed decision, to select the bank and account type, most suitable for them.

Some points to consider before selecting account type:

- What will be the source of your funds to deposit in India?
- Repatriation requirement of your money.
- Joint account preference with a parent or relative in India.
- Rental income in India and periodic bill payments in India.
- Consider not only the interest rate but also the conversion loss/gain in the long run.
- Interest received on some accounts like NRO account is subject to taxes in India, as well as abroad where you may reside. NRE account interest income though not taxable in India may be taxable in your home country.

♦ ♦ ♦

Deposit Insurance on NRI accounts in Indian Banks

Deposit insurance for accounts opened in Indian Banks by NRIs residing abroad, are NOT covered by foreign deposit insurance schemes in their country of residence.

United States
Non-Resident deposits with any Bank in India are not insured by Federal Deposit Insurance Corporation (FDIC) of the U.S.A.

Canada
Non-Resident deposits with any Bank in India are not insured by the Canadian Deposit Insurance Corporation (CDIC)

UK
Non-Resident deposits with any Bank in India are not protected under the UK Financial Services and Markets Act 2000, including the UK Financial Services Compensation Scheme.

Deposit insurance for bank accounts at Indian banks are provided by the Deposit Insurance and Credit Guarantee Corporation (DICGC).

However they do NOT offer insurance coverage to a few types of deposits, one of them is: 'Any amount due on account of any deposit received outside India'

When NRIs open non-resident bank accounts with various banks, they should read and understand the disclosure provided on the account opening forms.

Deposit insurance of their home countries may not apply to their foreign bank accounts.

Comparing NRO and NRE accounts

NRO	NRE
Maintained in Indian Rupees	Maintained in Indian Rupees
Interest is taxable	Tax free in India
Repatriation technically not allowed except on some types of deposits	Repatriation freely allowed of both principal and accrued interest
Can be jointly held with Indian citizen.	Cannot be jointly held with Indian citizen.

NRO account is useful for NRIs who are have income in India in Rupees, such as rental income, dividend income, pensions etc. Such an account can also be used to make payments in India for various bills like property taxes in India or for funds during visits to India.

NRE accounts are mainly for those who require repatriation facility for their money in India. This type of account is also free of tax in India. Deposits to both, NRE and NRO accounts can be sent from abroad or made in India.

Normally, most non-residents will need both NRO and NRE accounts. Money can be kept in NRE accounts and transferred to NRO as per requirements of the account holder.

♦♦♦

How to transfer funds from NRO to NRE Account

The announcement by the Reserve Bank of India, allowing repatriable funds to be transferred from NRO to NRE accounts, was welcomed by NRIs as good news. Prior to May 2012 the transfer of funds from NRO to NRE accounts was not allowed by The Reserve Bank of India.

Funds held in NRE accounts are tax free and easily repatriable. RBI now allows transfer from NRO account to NRE within the limit of US$ 1 million per financial year.

Documents that banks will require to initiate for such transfers, may differ slightly from bank to bank, as some banks may have some declaration forms in their own format. Generally the documents required are:

- Letter to the bank requesting transfer from NRO account to NRE account.
- FEMA Declaration Form – Your bank or CA can provide this one page form. This is basically your declaration that you are within your one million dollar limit in the financial year.
- Documentary evidence of source of funds
- Form 15CB [get this from a chartered accountant]
- Form 15CA
    - Step by step Information on how to access and fill Form 15CA is provided in this book under the heading 'What is Form 15CA'
- Once Form 15CA is filled, verify and submit
- Go to My account-My Returns/Forms. It will show all the returns and the Forms submitted.

- Click on the 15CA form and take a printout along with acknowledgement Slip.
- Form 15CA duly printed should be signed by Remitter and submitted to Bank in duplicate.

Some banks like the State Bank of India have forms in their own format to transfer funds from NRO to NRE.

Joint accounts with local residents

There are times when a non-resident may wish to have a joint account with an Indian resident, such as a family member for the sake of convenience.

Guidelines for having joint accounts in India are:

- NRE accounts cannot be held jointly with residents.
- NRO accounts can be held as joint accounts with Indian resident.
- NRIs/PIO holding NRE accounts can hold such accounts jointly only with other NRIs

Holding Foreign Currency Accounts in India

Persons of Indian origin, who do not wish to convert their foreign currency into Indian Rupees, by depositing money in NRE accounts, can open FCNR accounts.

Foreign currency non-resident (FCNR) accounts can be held in several foreign currencies such as, US dollars, GBP, Euro, Japanese Yen, Australian dollars or Canadian dollars.

♦♦♦

Difference between NRE and FCNR Account

- Deposits made to NRE accounts are converted to Indian Rupees, using the applicable rate of conversion on the day of the deposit. When a withdrawal is made in foreign currency from abroad, the money is reconverted back. Depending on the currency exchange rate at the time of withdrawal, the account holder may gain or lose money.
- FCNR accounts while they are maintained in the foreign currency of your choice cannot be used as current or savings accounts. FCNR accounts can only be maintained as 'term deposits' ranging from periods of one year to five years.

When account holders of FCNR accounts return to India as permanent residents, FCNR deposits they already hold will continue to pay interest at the contracted rate till maturity date of the deposit.

♦ ♦ ♦

Depositing foreign currency in NRE accounts

Banks allow account holders of NRE accounts, to make cash deposits in foreign currency notes or by traveler's cheque, to their NRE accounts when they are visiting India. However, there are two conditions that exist when it comes to such deposits.

- Deposited cash in foreign exchange should not exceed US$5000.
- In cases where the amount exceeds US$5000, a copy of a Currency Declaration Form is required.

This is to abide by Indian laws. Currency declaration Form acts as proof that the currency, was indeed brought into India from abroad by the person making the deposit.

Foreign currency declaration form requirement

Travelers can legally bring any amount of foreign exchange they wish into India. However, some conditions apply.

Indian law requires every passenger arriving in the country from overseas, to make a currency declaration to the Indian Customs at the time of arrival in India in case:

1. The value of foreign currency notes they are carrying exceeds US$ 5000/- or equivalent
2. If the aggregate value of foreign exchange (in the form of currency notes, bank notes, traveler cheque etc. exceeds US$ 10,000/- or its equivalent

Using Indian Bank Accounts to earn more interest

NRE accounts are fully repatriable and probably pay a slightly higher rate of interest, when compared to some foreign banks abroad. However, sometimes the rate of conversion and re-conversion can lower your final return.

NRE accounts take in foreign currency, convert it to Indian Rupees as per market rate and pay you tax free interest. When the account holder decides to repatriate the money abroad, it has to be re-converted to the original foreign currency at the rate of exchange prevalent at that time.

If the Indian Rupee value has fallen against the foreign currency then the account holder will suffer a loss.

Example:
Mr. Sharma, deposits $10,000 in an NRE account from New York. The rate of exchange when deposit is made is @55 Rupees to a dollar. The amount of Rupees 5, 50,000 is deposited in his account. The interest rate on his deposit is 4%.

After one year, Mr. Sharma decides to withdraw his money from his NRE account. He asks his bank, to send his money to his bank in New York. His original deposit was Rs. 5, 50,000 and with 4% interest, he would have received Rs. 22,000 as interest income. His total balance in the account would be Rs.5, 72,000.

Suppose the rate of exchange at that time of withdrawal is 65 Rupees for a dollar. His account balance of Rs. 5, 72,000 now converted to US$ = $8800 a loss of $1200 after earning 4% interest!

When opening NRE accounts, with the idea of repatriating your money, keep in mind that the interest received on the money should be high enough, to offset the rate of conversion and provide a reasonable gain as interest on the money deposited.

It is not easy to forecast rates of exchange in foreign currency; however an informed decision should be taken. In case the value of Indian Rupee in the example mentioned above goes up, Mr. Sharma would definitely benefit.

Even though interest generated on NRE bank accounts is tax free in India, the account holder may have to declare interest income on NRE accounts in their home country.

Exchange Earner's Foreign Currency Account

Exchange Earners' Foreign Currency Account (EEFC) is an account that can be maintained in foreign currency. EEFC accounts can be opened with a bank in India, by any Indian resident or company that has foreign exchange earnings.

EEFC accounts help their account holders avoid frequent foreign currency exchange fluctuations as no conversion of money is involved every time they send or receive money in foreign currency.

International Credit Cards

There are generally two types of credit cards issued by Indian banks.

1. Domestic credit card that is valid only in India.
2. International credit card.

Indian citizens can now get a domestic or international credit card from their banks. Issuance of credit cards would naturally depend on the assessment of their financial status, earning capacity and assets. All banks have their own criteria of evaluating credit card applications. RBI permission is generally not a requirement to get an international credit card.

International credit cards can be used while traveling abroad and also to pay for small services such as paying for a magazine subscription or domain hosting services on the internet.

Authorized dealer banks have been permitted by Reserve Bank of India to issue International Credit Cards to NRIs/PIO, without prior approval of RBI. In case a person of Indian origin wants to get a credit card that is valid in India only, they can do so. There are occasions when persons of Indian origin visiting India, will find that a local credit card actually does come in handy, for instance when making online reservations on railways and airlines.

Quite often in India, an Indian credit card is accepted while a foreign bank issued credit card may be declined by automatic authorizing terminals in India.

If your international Indian credit card is linked to your non-resident bank accounts such as NRE account, you may even be able to use that card abroad. Payments for such credit card transactions can be settled by inward remittance or out of balances held in your NRE bank account.

Tax deduction at source by Indian banks (TDS)

Interest earned on NRO Savings Account and NRO Fixed Deposits, is subject to tax deduction by the bank where your account is held. As of Aug 2009, applicable TDS rates for NRO accounts are set at 30.90%.

Persons of Indian origin, can however get a benefit under the DTAA and have only 15% TDS deducted, however to get this benefit they need to provide a tax residency certificate from the country whose citizenship they hold.

Information on 'How to get tax residency certificate' is provided in this book on page 102.

♦ ♦ ♦

Money Laundering Prevention Rules in India

Money laundering has become a way of not only trying to cheat on taxes, but to finance illegal activities. Identity theft, fraud and terrorist financing are a concern that everyone shares. Polices to prevent money laundering, have become a priority for governments across the globe.

In an effort to combat money laundering in India, the government has issued guidelines to banking institutions, to be on guard to track the movement of money that appears suspicious. Know you customer (KYC) is a requirement for most banks across the world.

Know your customer (KYC)

The Reserve Bank of India (RBI) has issued circulars and guidelines to Indian banks to ensure that they follow the KYC guidelines.

KYC guidelines require all Indian banks to be vigilant when opening new bank accounts. Under the 'know your customer' guidelines, Indian banks, when opening new accounts, are required to verify the identity and address of their customers.

Proof of Legal name to open bank account

As per RBI guidelines, any of the following are acceptable:

- Passport
- PAN Card
- Voter identity card
- Driving license
- Other Identity card (subject to the bank's satisfaction)

- Letter from recognized public authority or public servant verifying the identity and residence of the customer to the satisfaction of the bank

Acceptable Proof of Permanent Address

Any one of the following:

- Telephone bill
- Bank account statement
- Letter from recognized public authority
- Electricity bill
- Ration card
- Letter from employer (subject to the bank's satisfaction)

Bank customers categorized

Banks as part of KYC, normally categorize customers into low, medium and high risk, according to risk perceived.

Payments in cash

Cash payments of over Rupees 50,000 in India may cause problems. In a scenario where an account holder issues a bearer cheque to a third party for a sum over Rupees 50,000, the bank may refuse to cash it. Such payments need to made, by cross cheque, so they can track who the money is going to.

People do get around the Rupees 50,000 cash deposit ceiling by splitting the deposit into two separate transactions. NRIs however, should be aware that such a ceiling exists when it comes to cash dealings of Rs.50, 000 or more.

Status of NRO/NRE accounts on return to India

NRIs who return to India for settlement, are obligated to notify their banks of the change in their residential status, and get their accounts changed from non-resident bank accounts to resident bank accounts.

NRO accounts can be converted to regular Indian bank accounts and normally funds from NRE accounts can be deposited in a Resident Foreign Currency Account (RFC) account, which can be maintained in currencies such as USD, GBP, JPY and EURO.

Persons of Indian nationality or Indian origin, who have been resident outside India, for a continuous period of at least one year and then become residents of India, are allowed by the Reserve Bank of India to open and maintain RFC accounts in India. RFC accounts can be opened in any freely convertible foreign currency.

Deposit Insurance in India on bank accounts

All commercial banks, including branches of foreign banks that function in India, are insured by the Deposit Insurance and Credit Guarantee Corporation (DICGC).

DICGC protects bank deposits that are payable in India. In case of a bank failure of an insured bank, each depositor in a bank is insured up to a maximum of Rs.1, 00,000. Deposits that are kept in different branches of a bank are combined for the purpose of insurance cover and a maximum amount up to Rupees one lakh is paid.

While accounts in different branches of the same bank are combined for deposit insurance purposes, In case an individual has deposits with different banks, deposit insurance coverage limit is applied separately to the deposits in each bank.

Bank deposits **NOT** insured in India by DICGC

- Deposits of Foreign Governments
- Deposits of Central/State Governments
- Inter-Bank Deposits
- Deposits of the State Land Development Banks with the State Co-Operative Bank
- **Any amount due on account of deposit received outside India**
- Any amount, which has been specifically exempted by the Corporation with the previous approval of Reserve Bank of India.

♦♦♦

Deposit Insurance Comparison

Regardless of how foreign based NRIs look at it, the deposit insurance for bank accounts held in India is only Rupees one lakh per account. This works out to approximately US$ 1600.

In the United States of America, bank account deposits are insured by the Federal Deposit Insurance Corporation (FDIC). The standard insurance amount is $250,000 per depositor, per insured bank, for each account ownership category.

In Canada, the 'Canadian Deposit Insurance Corporation' (CDIC) insurance amount is $100,000. In UK up to £85,000 per person is covered.

NRI accounts held abroad are usually NOT covered under the

deposit insurance schemes available in foreign countries. NRIs/PIO wishing to bank in India should ensure that they deal with reputable banks.

Be aware that some co-operative credit societies may offer higher interest rates to attract customers. However, some of these may not be licensed by the authorities to operate as banks in India.

Bank Accounts-India-FAQ

Q. Can a foreign citizen of Indian origin, open a foreign currency account when they return to India for settlement with OCI?

A. Non-Residents Indians who have returned to India, can open a Resident Foreign Currency (RFC) account in India. RFC accounts can be opened in foreign currencies such as GBP, USD, JPY or EURO. If you decide to go abroad again you can transfer your funds to NRE/FCNR account. RFC accounts are repatriable.

Q. Can any Indian resident open resident foreign currency account in India?

A. Persons of Indian nationality or origin who have been resident outside India for a continuous period of at least one year can open RFC accounts.

In case a persons who returns to India after an absence of less than one year and wants to open a RFC account to deposit foreign currency. They are required to seek RBI permission to open RFC account. This is done by applying to RBI through the bank where they wish to open RFC account, on the appropriate form.

Q. Can a resident in India, open a foreign currency account for business purposes?

A. Indian residents who are engaged in a business that earns foreign exchange are allowed to open foreign currency account in India. Reserve Bank of Indian (RBI) allows the opening of an account called 'Exchange Earners Foreign Currency Account' (EEFC).

Q. I am a foreign citizen now living in India, can a foreign national resident in India open a local bank account or must I open a NRO account?

A. Yes! Foreign citizens, who are resident in India, can open a resident bank account, as any other citizen of India. Regardless of what citizenship a person has, if they are resident in India legally, they can open a regular bank account.

Q. Can a foreign tourist visiting India open a bank account in India.

A. Yes! Foreign tourists visiting India can open a bank account in India. Funds are held in Indian currency. The maximum period of holding such an account is six months.

Q. Can a foreign citizen of Indian origin make a cash deposit in US$ to his NRE bank account in India?

A. Yes! Foreign currency notes can be deposited by a foreign citizen of Indian origin in their NRE account, subject to a limit of US$ 5000 or its equivalent. Foreign currency in excess of US$5000 is allowed only on production of a Currency Declaration Form (CDF).

CDF is issued by the customs authorities when passengers on arrival make a currency declaration to declare the amount of currency they are bringing into India.

Q. Do all foreign nationals have to make a currency declaration when they arrive in India?

A. No, the Currency declaration form need not be completed in cases where the aggregate value of the foreign exchange brought in by the passenger in the form of currency notes, bank notes, or travelers cheque does not exceed U.S.$ 10,000/- or the value of foreign currency notes brought in does not exceed U.S.$ 5,000 or its equivalent.

Q. I am a resident in USA; can I send a power of attorney to my relative in India to open a NRE account for me?

A. Opening of NRE accounts for others by way of holding POA is not allowed.

Q. I have a non-resident account with a bank in India, as I live in Dubai can I make this a joint account with my father so that he can operate it for convenience.

A. If you have a NRE account, you cannot make this a joint account. However, if you have a NRO account, then you can jointly hold this type of account with your father or any other person.

Non-residents can hold both types of accounts in India. Hence, if you currently only have an NRE account you can also open a NRO account and make this a joint account.

Q. Is the interest on NRO account repatriable? Some say it is and others say that it is not, pointing out that only NRE account interest is repatriable.

A. For NRO accounts, interest became repatriable from the financial year 1994-1995. Interest on NRO accounts is now repatriable.

Q. When a non-resident returns to India, what happens to the NRE and NRO accounts they already hold in India?

A. Banks holding the accounts should be advised of the change in residential status of the account holder and banks should then re-designate the accounts to resident accounts.

Q. When I opened a NRO account several years ago my bank told me the money would not be repatriable. Is money held in NRO accounts now repatriable?

A. Technically funds held in NRO accounts are not repatriable, only the interest can be repatriated. However depending on the source of the money deposited in the account, for example sale proceeds of property, can be repatriated under RBI scheme that allows persons of Indian origin to remit up to One million USD per calendar year out of balances held in their NRO account.

Q. I am a foreign passport holder of Indian origin settled in Australia; I inherited a house in India and now I am selling it. Can the money from the sale of this house be sent to my foreign bank account?

A. Yes! Sale proceeds of assets acquired through inheritance can be transferred abroad. The money must first be deposited in your NRO account and then it can be sent abroad after providing proof that the money is indeed from the sale of inherited property and any taxes due, have been paid.

Q. Must pension income received from overseas by a resident in India be deposited in a resident Rupee account?

A Pension income that is received from overseas can be deposited in Resident Foreign Currency account.

Q. Must NRIs pay hotel bills in foreign currency when visiting India?

A. Hotel bills can be paid by NRIs in Indian rupees.

Q. What happens to RFC account if account holder decides to go abroad?

A. RFC account proceeds are fully repatriable.

Investing in the Indian Stock Market

The first step to invest in the Indian markets is to open a Demat account. NRIs do not require permission from the Reserve Bank of India (RBI) to open a Demat account.

Basically, an NRI needs to have a bank account, a Demat account, and a 'Portfolio Investment Scheme' (PIS) account to start investing. Those NRIs who already have a NRO or NRE account can ask their banks for a PIS application and submit it to them for opening a 'Portfolio Investment Scheme' (PIS) account.

What exactly is a Demat account

Simply explained, a Demat account, is similar to a bank account. While money is held in bank accounts, securities in electronic form are held in Demat accounts.

Demat Accounts for NRIs - PIO

An investment by a foreign national of Indian origin (PIO) in Indian securities is treated the same way as an investment by non-resident Indian citizens. NRIs and PIO can open a Demat account with any depository participant (DP). Most banks are authorized Depository Participants.

The definition of PIO

A 'Person of Indian Origin' means an individual (not being a citizen of Pakistan or Bangladesh or Sri Lanka or Afghanistan or China or Iran or Nepal or Bhutan) who at any time,

- *held an Indian Passport or*
- *who or either of whose father or mother or whose*

grandfather or grandmother was a citizen of India by virtue of the Constitution of India or the Citizenship Act, 1955 (57 of 1955).

Demat Accounts - Information for NRIs

- When a person becomes an NRI and already holds resident Demat account in India. They are required to close the Demat accounts held prior to becoming an NRI and open a NRO Demat account. They can then transfer the shares they held in the previous Demat account into this new NRO Demat account.
- While they can continue to hold shares in their NRO Demat account or sell them when they prefer, they cannot purchase more shares from the secondary market for this account.
  They can however; purchase shares from the primary market through their NRO Demat account.
  If they sell any shares held in their NRO Demat Account, the sale proceeds must be deposited into a NRO Savings Account.
- NRIs, who wish to buy shares from the secondary market, are required to open a PIS account with a bank of their choice. When opening a PIS account, also open a NRE and NRO account. RBI has specified that an NRI must have a separate account linked to the PIS account. It cannot be the NRO or NRE account through which other routine transactions are conducted.
- Shares bought with funds from NRE accounts and sale proceeds of such shares, can then be credited to the NRE

account and are fully repatriable. Shares bought and sold on non-repatriable basis can use NRO account.

- Only one PIS account with one bank can be opened. If you have an account with one bank, you cannot open such an account with another bank.

RBI approvals to open Demat accounts

For non-resident Indians and persons of Indian origin (PIO), there is no approval required from the RBI to open a Demat account in India. However all NRI buy/sell transactions in the secondary market, on any stock exchange in India, must be done under the Portfolio Investment Scheme (PIS) as per the regulations under the Foreign Exchange Management Act (FEMA). NRIs can register for secondary market transactions under the PIS with only one authorized dealer.

Types of Demat accounts

For NRIs, there are two types of Demat Accounts.

- Repatriable
- Non-Repatriable

Repatriable Demat Account

Repatriable Demat accounts are for holding shares and securities that are legally allowed to be repatriated.

Shares that can be legally repatriated are those purchased by using funds from accounts that are designated as repatriable, for example NRE accounts. When you sell shares held in a repatriable Demat account, the sale proceeds can be credited to your NRE Bank account. All money held in NRE accounts is fully repatriable.

Non-Repatriable Demat Account

This type of account is for holding shares and securities that have been purchased by using funds that are not repatriable. For example shares purchased from an NRO account.

Shares sold from non-repatriable Demat accounts, cannot be repatriated and the money from the sale of such shares, can be credited to your NRO Bank account.

Paper stocks already held

If you already hold the paper stock certificates, they must now be dematerialized before they can be sold.

What does dematerialization of stocks mean?

The process by which paper share certificates you hold, are converted to an electronic record. The shares when dematerialized, will then reflect as a credit in your Demat account.

How to dematerialize paper shares

Submit the physical share certificates, along with a duly filled dematerialized form to your Depository Participant (Where you hold Demat account). Proof of acquisition, such as allotment letter, may also be required.

The process after documentation is submitted, can take about a month as certificates first have to be verified.

Don't submit physical shares, without knowing who you are

giving these to. Common sense is advised; don't deal with self-proclaimed share brokers but authorized banks only.

Re-materialization

If you ever decide that you want your certificates back, you can submit a request, by filling the 'Re-materialization Request Form'

Investments, shares, debentures & mutual funds

NRIs are allowed to make direct investments, in shares/ debentures of Indian companies/units of mutual funds. They can also make portfolio investments, such as purchase of shares/debentures of Indian companies through stock exchange.

♦♦♦

Portfolio Investment Scheme (PIS)

PIS is a scheme of the Reserve Bank of India, that allows NRIs and persons of Indian origin, to purchase and sell shares and convertible debentures of Indian Companies, on a recognized stock exchange in India, by routing all purchase or sale transactions through their account, held with a Designated Bank Branch.

NRIs or PIO who wish to make investments; trades in the Indian Equity Secondary Market are required to have a PIS account with a designated bank in India. PIS account is applicable only for NRIs/PIO and not for resident Indians.

General Information about PIS account

- PIS account is only for trading in Indian markets and not for any other foreign markets.
- Applicable only for equity trades and not MF investments.

Why PIS required by NRIs and PIO

Indian companies have certain limits set for foreign investment and such limits are monitored under current FEMA regulations. Companies cannot exceed the foreign investment limits set. There is no standard set limit for foreign investments and the limit set by the authorities are different for each company.

It should also be noted that no NRI or PIO is not allowed to invest more than 5% in any Indian company. This is one of the reasons; NRIs cannot simply go online to conduct transactions directly. They have to route all purchase or sale transactions, through their account held with a Designated Bank Branch, as limits have to be monitored under FEMA regulations, to ensure a company's foreign investment limit has not exceeded.

Non-PIS Account

Non-PIS account is a normal savings bank account and can be opened with any bank in India. These accounts are used for transactions that are not required to be reported to RBI. Non PIS account can be NRO or NRE.

The following are some of the transactions allowed under Non-PIS accounts:

- Sale of shares, which were, acquired other than PIS.
- Shares acquired through Initial Public Offerings.
- Gifts from relatives or otherwise.
- Shares bought as resident Indian.
- Fresh acquisition through IPO's.
- Investment in Mutual Funds

Portfolio Investment Scheme FAQ

Q. What is the Portfolio Investment Scheme?

A. This is a scheme under which, Non-residents are allowed to acquire shares/debentures of Indian companies through the stock exchanges in India.

Q. How is a PIS account opened?

A. Reserve Bank of India has authorized dealers, such as banks, to conduct business under the portfolio investment scheme. Approach your financial institution to make an application for a PIS account.

Q. Is RBI permission required to be sought by PIS account opener?

A. No permission is required.

Q. Can applications for PIS be made to more than one designated bank?

A. Only one is allowed, select the bank of your choice.

Q. Do I need to open a bank account in the bank where I make an application for PIS account?

A Yes, this makes operations easier. Open NRO or NRE account depending on the investment being repatriable or non-repatriable. Both these accounts can be opened at your bank you may be currently dealing with.

While only one PIS account is allowed, NRIs can open more than one NRO or NRE accounts

♦♦♦

Investing in Initial Public Offerings

NRI investment in IPO's does not come under PIS. Such investments are covered under the Reserve Bank of India's Foreign Direct Investment Regulations.

NRIs do not require any permission to invest in IPO's as the Issuing Company must follow all necessary regulations, for issuing securities to a person resident outside India.

NRI investments in government securities

Investments can be made by NRIs in Government securities or Units of Unit Trust of India (UTI). Investment can be made through authorized dealers.

Investing in National Savings Certificates

NRIs are allowed to invest in National Savings Certificates as per terms set for the sale of such certificates when released.

Investment in 100% Export Oriented Units

NRIs are permitted to invest up to 100% in such units subject to prior approval from the Ministry of Industries.

Investments prohibited for NRIs

NRIs are not permitted to invest in securities such as:

- Kisan Vikas Patra
- Indira Vikas Patra
- Public Provident Fund (PPF) – [Can continue with account if opened prior to becoming NRI]

Securities & Exchange Board of India - NRI Cell

To offer assistance to NRIs and address concerns of NRI investors, the Securities and Exchange Board of India has created a separate 'NRI cell' at the SEBI Head Office in Mumbai.

The purpose of the SEBI-NRI Cell is to provide redressal of the problems faced by NRI investors, in their dealings involving the Indian securities markets.

The following is an explanatory list of the types of complaints, grievances that an NRI investor may have against a listed company, which they can take up with the NRI cell of SEBI for appropriate redressal.

- Non receipt of refund orders/allotment letters/stock investments.
- Non receipt of dividend.
- Non receipt of share certificates/bonus shares.
- Non receipt of debenture certificates/interest/redemption amount/interest on delayed payment of interest on debentures.

Here is the link for The Securities and Exchange Board of India: http://www.sebi.gov.in/annualreport/9697/pt3l.html

Precautions for Investment in Securities

When it comes to investing in shares/securities in India, NRIs should invest after doing proper research.

- Make sure your broker is registered with SEBI, don't deal with unregistered intermediaries.

- Confirm that the company you are contemplating to invest in, has filed its offer documents with SEBI.
- Ensure that the company has taken the required Government and Reserve Bank of India approvals.
- Take informed decisions by studying the fundamentals of the company. Check the past track record of the company by looking at annual reports.
- Don't invest based on hot tips! Many NRIs are misled by market rumors or luring advertisements.
- Find an investment advisor if you prefer BUT use common sense in decision making. Advisors, brokers may have a tendency to steer clients to where they make the most commission.
- Past performance of a company, should be taken only as a guideline; there is no guarantee whatsoever of future performance.
- Don't invest money you can't afford to lose!
- Any NRI, who has invested in listed companies and has complaints, can now approach SEBI to take up their grievances, against such companies thorough SEBI NRI Cell.

♦♦♦

Reverse Mortgages - India

Reverse mortgages have been around in the western world for some time now, but are relatively new in India. This type of mortgage allows senior homeowners to use their home equity to get cash payments periodically, so they can live comfortably in their own home, during their lifetime.

In India reverse mortgages are offered to senior citizens who are over 60 years of age. If such a senior owns a house, they can mortgage their property with a lender and convert part of the home equity into tax-free income, without having to sell the house.

Instead of you making monthly payments to a lender as with a regular home loan, the senior citizen receives payments from the lender. This type of mortgage is ideal for senior citizens who have homes but not enough income to live a comfortable life. The payments they receive are also tax free.

Married couples can be eligible as joint borrowers for such loans. While the criteria of qualification would depend on the lending institution, to qualify, one of them should be above 60 years of age and the other not below 55 years of age.

Senior citizens seeking such mortgages should be using their property as a permanent primary residence. The loan is normally serviced as long as the borrower is alive and in occupation of the property. The loan is repaid through sale of property after the borrower's death.

When the property is eventually sold, any amount remaining after the loan is paid off, will go to legal heirs.

The amount of money seniors can get, depends on their age, the value of their property and prevailing interest rates.

Why Reverse Mortgages not successful in India

After being offered in India since 2006, reverse mortgages have not seen many seniors take advantage of this scheme. Perhaps the reason are:

- Lack of awareness of this type of mortgage amongst seniors
- For some seniors it might be a matter of ethics that they wish to pass on their property to their loved ones.
- The payout by banks is generally offered for a term of 15 to 20 years.
- Children of such seniors may not like the idea of their parents mortgaging property which they hope to own some day!

Loans for NRIs

Housing loans in India are now becoming a popular method to finance the purchase of homes in India. Indian financial institutions, now also offer reverse mortgages for senior citizens. Reverse mortgages is a concept that enables senior citizens who own a house ,to mortgage their property with a lender and convert part of the home equity into tax-free income; without having to sell their house.

Housing loans in India

As real-estate prices go up steadily, many professionals with good salaries, but no savings are utilizing housing loans to purchase property. One of the questions NRIs/PIO may have is, whether they can avail housing loans to purchase property in India.

The Reserve bank of India has permitted authorized dealers, such as banks in India, to provide housing loans to NRIs basically on the same rules applicable to residents. Normally banks will finance up to 85% of the purchase price.

There are however, some rules that must be followed when providing loans to non-resident Indians and persons of Indian origin who are resident outside India.

Conditions applicable to housing loans for NRIs

- Housing loan amount given to non-residents cannot be deposited to any non-resident type of bank account, such as, NRE account or an FCNR account.
- Such loans must be fully secured by equitable mortgages of

the property being acquired with the loan. A lien on the borrowers other assets, held in India can also be included by the financing institution.

Repayment of housing loans by non-residents

NRIs can pay off housing loans in India from abroad through normal banking channels. Payments can also be made from funds held in NRO, NRE or FCNR accounts. Even rental income from the property can be utilized to make loan payments.

Housing Loans from employer

Foreigners of Indian origin who are employed in India by a company registered or incorporated in India, may also be able to get housing loans from their employers.

Renovation Loans for NRI/PIO

The Reserve Bank of India vide its Circular No. 95 under the A.P. (DIR Series) dated April 26, 2003, has also clarified that housing finance institutions, may also grant loans to NRIs/PIO for the purpose of repairs/renovation/improvement of residential properties owned by them in India.

Business Loans for Returning NRIs

Business loans are available to non-residents returning to India to setup new businesses. OCI holders are normally treated at par with other Indian citizens when it comes to getting loans. The same rules and interest rates applicable to residents, also apply to OCI holders in India. NRIs do not have to pay more nor are they given discounts.

Each loan case is approved on the basis of the applicant's

personal investment, their business experience and background. Normally, an entrepreneur is expected to put up 25% of the capital required for a project, the rest can be financed. This figure of course would depend on the lending institution on a case by case basis.

Hundred percent loans for new business

There is no such thing as a 100% loan in India. Banks will only provide loans for new businesses that have collateral. The only exception here would be loans under 'Government of India launched Credit Guarantee Scheme'.

New business ventures would probably have no track record of success and banks are reluctant to finance brand new projects, unless the entrepreneur is investing their own money up front, to show that they are serious about their business plan.

Business Loans & Financial Assistance

Financial assistance for entrepreneurs in India is provided by:

- State Financial Corporations.
- National small industries corporation (NSIC)
- State Directorates of Industries
- Commercial Banks.
- Industrial Development Bank of India.
- Regional Rural Banks also provide financial assistance to small scale industry sectors.

Credit Guarantee Scheme (MSME)

Government of India launched Credit Guarantee Scheme (CGS) in an effort to help small, entry level entrepreneurs get access to business loans from banks.

Many startup businesspersons are unable to get business loans from banks, as they usually don't have collateral and banks consider lending new entrepreneurs a risky business.

This scheme basically, provides a guarantee for the major part of the loan made to business persons. The Scheme covers collateral free loans from eligible lending institutions, to new and existing micro and small enterprises, of up to Rupees 100 lakh per borrowing unit.

The main benefit of this scheme is that the borrower does not have to provide any collateral or third party guarantee for getting this type of loan. The lending institutions are expected to give loans, based on the viability of the project and secure the loan amount, on the primary security of the assets financed.

The government provides the lending institutions with a guarantee that covers up to 75% - 80% of the sanctioned amount of the loan. The maximum guarantee coverage is of Rs.62.50 lakh / Rs. 65 lakh. The extent of guarantee cover is 85% for micro enterprises for credit up to Rs.5 lakh.

What are Micro & Small Enterprises?

In case you are wondering what is classified as a Micro or Small enterprise, the classification is based on the valuation of the enterprise. According to the Micro, Small and Medium Enterprises (MSME) Development Act of 2006:

Manufacturing Enterprise

- A micro enterprise is where the investment in plant and machinery, does not exceed twenty five lakh rupees.
- A small enterprise is where the investment in plant and machinery, is more than twenty five lakh rupees but does not exceed five crore rupees.
- A medium enterprise, is where the investment in plant and machinery, is more than five crore rupees but does not exceed ten crore rupees.

Service Enterprise

In the case of enterprises that are engaged in providing or rendering of services, the valuation is slightly different.

- A micro enterprise for service enterprise is where the investment in equipment does not exceed ten lakh rupees.
- A small enterprise for service enterprise is where the investment in equipment, is more than ten lakh rupees but does not exceed two crore rupees.
- A medium enterprise for the service sector, is where the investment in equipment is more than two crore rupees but does not exceed five crore rupees.

Who is eligible for loans & where to apply

New and existing Micro and Small Enterprises engaged in manufacturing or service can apply for such loans. However, those engaged in the 'Retail Trade' are not eligible for loans under this scheme. Most banks can be approached for such loans. A complete list of member lending institutions is available at: http://www.cgtmse.com/List_Of_MLIs.aspx

New Industry setup in India

Those who want to setup an Industrial venture, have a great opportunity to do so in India. While setting up a new industry in India is no easy task, it can prove to be very rewarding for those who are willing to work hard to achieve their goals.

Finding the right type of professionals for your project, getting a project report made, preparing business plans for financing etc. can cost quite a bit of money and time, especially for people who have been out of the country for some period of time. Fortunately, some help is provided for new entrepreneurs, by various government departments.

Governments help for new entrepreneurs

Entrepreneurs can seek help from Ministry of Micro, Small and Medium Enterprises (MSME). New entrepreneurs can get excellent guidance for their projects in a cost effective manner from MSME.

MSME development help

The Micro, Small & Medium Enterprises can help in the promotion and development of Micro, Small and Medium Enterprises. Some of the helpful services provided to entrepreneurs are:

- Assistance/Consultancy to Prospective Entrepreneurs.
- Assistance/Consultancy to existing Micro and Small Enterprises.
- Preparation of Project Reports/Project Profiles.

- Entrepreneurship Development Programs
- Motivation Campaigns.
- Project Appraisal for Bank/Financial Institutions.
- Management Development Programs.
- Skill Development Programs.
- Awareness Programs on Energy Conservation/Pollution Control.
- Quality Improvement & Technology upgradation.
- Export Promotion.
- Ancillary Development.
- Linkage with State Govt. Functionaries.
- Market Surveys.
- Marketing Support through NSIC Enlistment by giving Technical Inspection Report.
- Registration of Micro and Small Enterprises under Ozone Depleting Substances (Regulation & Control) Rules, 2000.

Here is the website link for an overview of MSME http://www.dcmsme.gov.in/ssiindia/MSME_OVERVIEW09.pdf

National Small Scale Industries Corporation (NSIC)

NSIC can offer help to small and medium scale industries by offering support for their promotion, aid and growth. They provide guidance to small and medium scale industry in India such as:

- Help in securing credit.
- Export insurance for small and medium industry for their products.
- Raw Material Assistance Scheme, aims at helping Small Scale Industries/Enterprises by way of financing the purchase of Raw Material. [http://www.nsic.co.in/rma.asp]
- National Small Industries Corporation (NSIC) is a recognized Export House and can help small industries with export of their products.
- Governments are usually big buyers of products & services. NSIC can help small-scale sector to sell their products to the Government.
- NSIC organizes and participates in domestic and specialized product & technology related international exhibitions, so as to help small scale industries in marketing their products and projects in both national and international markets.

NSIC can provide loads of information that is current and up to date. Entrepreneurs can get help to stay in touch with the market and business environment.

For additional information visit the National Small Industries Corporation (NSIC) website: http://www.nsic.co.in/index.asp

♦ ♦ ♦

NRI Business Opportunities

As priorities or economic situations change for Indian NRIs settled abroad, some may consider returning to India. One of the questions on the minds of such NRIs may be; to decide on what type of work or business they can pursue if they eventually did return to India.

Professionals, such as software engineers, doctors etc. Have a career path already laid out and need no help in deciding. However, not all NRIs have special skills, nor do they all have unlimited money. NRIs who decide to return to India, must have a carefully drafted plan to be able to successfully settle in India.

Business Setup in India

There are many advantages of setting up a business in India. The main advantage of starting a business in India is, that India in itself is a large market. Recent census reports indicate that India now has 1.21 billion people, 17% of the world's population today, are Indians! A smart businessman will setup shop where customers are, one of the largest customer base today, happens to be India.

Just about any item can be manufactured, however, for any business to be successful; they must be able to sell their products. This is where India's huge market is helpful. Multinational companies are in India today, because of the vast Indian market they can sell to.

The Indian economy is doing very well, despite depressed economic news from many western countries. Indians now have a fair chunk of disposable income and are prospering economically. Whether it is cars, electronics or household goods, there is a huge market in India.

India has an abundance of talent available for hire at reasonable costs. Family businesses, run by non-residents in many western cities, involve working endless hours of work. Labor is expensive in western countries. Entrepreneurs in India can well afford to hire extra workers, as labor costs in India are still quite low.

Business setup problems in India

While there may be advantages of having a business in India, setting up a new business, is actually no easy task for persons who have lived abroad for an extended period of time. If you plan to return to India to start a business, keep in mind that things are a lot different in India today, compared to what they were several years ago.

To start a new business in India, licensing requirements, dealing with labor, utilities, environment clearances etc. may have to be dealt with and in India, you can't do all this by simply using the telephone! NRIs who return to India for the purpose of setting up a business can succeed, if they are willing to adapt to the Indian psyche.

Setting up of a business organization in India

The main forms business organizations in India are:

- Companies (public & private)
- Partnerships
- Limited liability partnership
- Sole proprietorship

All companies that are incorporated in India, including branches of foreign corporations in India are regulated by the Companies Act 1956.

The Registrar of Companies and the Company Law Board work under the Ministry of Corporate Affairs and ensure compliance with the Act.

Description of companies

Characteristics of various types of companies is briefly provided here for informational purposes. NRIs should seek the help of professional CA/Lawyer in India if they are considering setting up a new business in India.

Private Limited Companies

As per Section 3(1) (iii) of the 'Companies Act, 1956, a private company is defined as one which:-

- Has a minimum paid-up capital of one lakh rupees or such higher paid-up capital as may be prescribed by its articles, and
- Restricts the right to transfer its shares, if any;
- limits the number of its members to 50 which will not include:-
  (1) members who are employees of the company; and
  (2) members who are ex-employees of the company and were members while in such employment and who have continued to be members after ceasing to be employees;
- Prohibits any invitation to the public to subscribe for any shares in, or debentures of, the company;

Public Company

As per Section 3(1) (IV) public company means a company which-

- Is not a private company;
- Has a minimum paid-up capital of five lakh rupees or such higher paid-up capital, as may be prescribed;
- Is a private company, which is a subsidiary of a company which is not a private company

Register a new company in India

Company registration in India, is regulated by the Companies Act, 1956 and is administered by the Ministry of Corporate Affairs through the Offices of Registrar of Companies (ROC) in each State.

Steps to register a new company

- Get an approved Digital Signature Certificate from the Ministry of Corporate Affairs (MCA) in India.
- Apply for a Director Identification Number (DIN) online. These are given out by the MCA.
- File an application with the Registrar of Companies (ROC) for a Company Name *(Name search to ensure that the name is available must be done)* the name will be approved if it adheres to the MCA's Guidelines for Name Availability.
- Draft a Memorandum of Association (MOA) and Articles of Association (AOA). These documents are required under the Companies Act.

- Obtain seal of validation for the documents. All of the first shareholders need to sign their names and include their fathers' name, address, and job title.
- Submit the documents to the ROC. The registrar will register your company

All forms and applications for acquiring digital signature etc. are available on the MCA website. Most of the formalities mentioned above can be done online from the Ministry of Corporate Affairs, Government of India website http://www.mca.gov.in

The registration process may sound confusing to a non-resident however; these are routine matters for a CA in India. Avail the services of a CA and get just about everything done in a timely manner. Although the online procedure is fairly simple, NRIs will save time by using a chartered accountant.

Registration process of small businesses

Normally national company registration is only required of corporations. Businesses such as a sole proprietorship, registrations are done at the local government level. Usually you would have to approach the local municipal offices.

For instance, to start a factory in Delhi, you would contact the Municipal Corporation of Delhi, factory licensing department http://www.mcdfactorylicense.in

Similarly; if you are planning to setup a small business in Mumbai, contact the Mumbai Municipal Corporation.

♦ ♦ ♦

Licenses & Approvals required for a small business

Regardless of the type of business one intends to start, some form of registration and licensing, from the appropriate authorities is required. Business registration is basically the creation of a legal entity, the best way for NRIs to proceed in such cases, is to contact a chartered accountant who can guide them and perhaps have the appropriate registration work done on their behalf.

To give readers an idea, of what is actually required in terms of business licensing in India, here is an example. Suppose a person wants to open a shop or restaurant in India, here are some of the things required:

1. Pan number registration for the business with the income tax department for filing annual returns.
2. Sales tax registration with the sales tax department.
3. Registration certificate of establishment with the Municipal ward office.
4. Fire Department clearance is required from the chief fire officer of the area.
5. Water connection certificate from the municipal water department.
6. To serve food and liquor a 'Health License' from the Municipal ward office Health Department is required.
7. State Excise and Prohibition License may be required from the Permit Room Excise Department.

8. Food & Drug Control Act License (FDA) Prevention of adulteration from the State Health Ministry.
9. Police Registration Certificate may be required for places such as a restaurant that is deemed as a place of public entertainment, from the Asst. Commissioner of Police.
10. Trade/Storage License Permission to conduct trade from the 'Office of the Municipal Commissioner'
11. Suppose you plan to play sound recorded music from cd's etc. in your new restaurant. You need to get a license from the Indian Performing Right Society (IPRS).
12. Pollution Clearance certificate from the City Engineer (Civil) – Environment Department.
13. Employee State Insurance Scheme (ESIS) certificate for shops and establishments employing more than ten staff.
14. For Restaurants, Health Certificate for kitchen staff from the Health Department.
15. Weights & Measurements Certificate Verification of weighing scales used on premises from the State Weights & Measurement Department.

Sounds complicated, however with help from your accountant and perhaps a lawyer, most of these things can be done in a timely and cost effective manner. On the other hand trying to get approvals and licensing, on your own, can be difficult, time consuming, frustrating and quite costly for most returning NRIs.

♦ ♦ ♦

Options on setting up business in India

To set up a business venture in India, returning non-residents normally have the option to:

1. Start a new business
2. Purchase a franchise.
3. Purchase a business that is already running.

Policies of the governments on the central, as well as state level in India are now quite business friendly. New entrepreneurs can take advantage of loans, grants and incentives offered by the various government agencies.

Business Ideas

When it comes to deciding what type of business to setup in India by a returning NRIs, the ideal business opportunity for them of course would be, to look for a similar business that they had been involved in during their stay overseas.

Regardless of the type of business chosen, setting up a new business in any part of the world involves financial resources, commitment and planning.

Some business suggestions are provided here.

- Franchise: Many successful franchises now have outlets in India. Most non-residents may already be aware of the success abroad of franchises such as, Subway, Kentucky fried chicken, Baskin Robbins to name a few.
- Horticulture: India has an excellent potential when it comes to horticulture. Some of the best flowers are exported from India and sent all over Europe.

- Call center: Online customer support for overseas companies.
- Poultry farming.
- Hotel Industry
- Medical X-ray, Medical testing laboratory, MRI . . .
- Investment in taxi business
- Distributor of products of popular companies
- Travel - Tourism

Franchising is probably the easiest method of setting up a business, just about anywhere in the world, and India is no exception. Non-residents, who have been away for quite some time from India, perhaps may not understand the Indian market. This is where opting for a franchise may beneficial.

Franchise Company generally provides help in usually every phase of startup, such as location selection, business setup, hiring and training of staff. This is one business concept that provides help from day one.

Benefits of Franchise

Most NRIs are probably familiar with international franchises; many internationally known franchises are now setup in India. Let's take an example of one such franchise, to get an idea about franchising in India.

Example:

Baskin Robbins is one of the World's leading brands of Ice Cream Parlors; they currently have a presence in more than 40 countries. They setup operations in India in 1993. Now they have franchises in 58 cities of India with 200 locations.

In India they offer a franchise in the form of Lounges, Cafes, Parlors and Kiosk. The required investment ranges from Rs Rs.800, 000 to Rs.2, 000,000 depending on format chosen.

There are many more companies that offer franchises that may interest prospective business men. Purchasing a franchise is probably the easiest route to starting a new business for non-residents who return to India.

In addition to internationally known franchises that can be quite expensive to start, there are many Indian franchises that offer excellent business opportunities. Getting a loan for a reputable franchise may also be a lot easier.

If you are considering purchase of a franchise in India, one of the best places to start in India is Franchise India, they have an excellent website, where you can get valuable information on franchising opportunities in India. Their website address is: http://www.franchiseindia.com

Another good place to start is Business Franchise, their website address is: http://www.franchisebusiness.in here you will find information on the various types of franchises that are available in India, as well as help in purchasing a franchise, that you may feel is suitable to you.

If you wish to probe the Indian market for a franchise opportunity, then these two companies can provide you with a lot of information, on national and international franchises that are available currently in India.

An added advantage of purchasing a franchise is that you can also check out other franchisees businesses, to see firsthand how their setup is and what income potential exists.

A lot of guess work is taken out of by purchasing a franchise. NRIs returning to India should consider checking out various franchising opportunities, if they are on the lookout for a new business opportunity in India.

Government incentives for New Business

For those who wish to setup a new manufacturing industry in India, help and incentives to setup a business, are available from state governments. Those wishing to start new manufacturing units can get help in the form of:

- Purchase of land at discounted prices.
- Industrial sheds in state industrial estates.
- Exemption from paying taxes for several years.
- Help in getting approval of required licensing from various authorities.

Depending on the State in India, where one wishes to setup new manufacturing facilities, State governments have their own set of incentives and grants and often compete with other states, for new businesses to be located in their state.

Setting up an Industry in India

For individual NRIs who wish to setup an industry in India, the best method of going forward may be to setup their project, under the small scale industry polices.

To help smaller manufacturers in India, the Indian Government, has reserved certain products for manufacture in the small scale sector. This helps protect smaller manufacturers, from larger corporations, who have a lot of money and small manufacturing unit owners would not be able to compete with them.

In the event Large/Medium units decide to manufacture items

reserved for small scale industry, they can do so provided; they undertake to export 50% or more of their production.

An industrial undertaking is defined as a small scale industry unit, if the investment in fixed assets such as machinery, whether held on ownership terms on lease or on hire purchase, does not exceed Rupees one crore (Rupees 10 million).

Setting up Industrial Unit in India

NRIs planning to setup an industrial unit, anywhere in India can get help and guidance by contacting the Council of State Industrial Development and Investment Corporations of India. They (COSIDICI) act as a facilitator for rendering assistance and guidance in respect of:

- Availability of loans on soft terms;
- Allotment of industrial plot/shed in one of the industrial estates or industrial parks developed by the state level corporation;
- Technical assistance for the preparation of project reports;
- Availability of special incentives provided by the respective state governments for setting up of industries, etc.

Those who are planning to set up an industrial unit in India can get help and guidance from the COSIDICI.

COSIDICI has a link with the concerned departments of State Governments, Central Government and Indian financial institutions. The affairs of COSIDICI are managed, by an executive committee consisting of senior civil servants drawn from various state level corporations. The composition of the executive committee is such, that all regions of the country are represented on it.

Those planning to set up an industrial unit, in the small, medium or large sector, anywhere in India should approach the COSIDICI.

The Council of State Industrial Development and Investment Corporations of India, publish a monthly newsletter with useful information for entrepreneurs. Their newsletter is available by subscription or you can read it free online at: **http://www.cosidici.com/newsletter-v.htm**

Incentive for Backward Areas

The government in an effort to help develop India's backward regions provides from time to time, special incentives and grants for business to setup in such designated areas. A list of backward districts specified by the Central Government is available at: http://www.dcmsme.gov.in/policies/bwrd.htm

State Government Incentives

Many state governments in India also have their own set of incentives for setting up industry. Some of the Incentives provided by state governments in India, for setting up new industry in their state, are provided for general knowledge purposes in this book.

Links to the government websites are also provided to help prospective entrepreneurs get current information as rules and regulations do change from time to time.

Incentives offered by State Government's

Just about every state government in India offers incentives to attract new business to setup in their state. This helps the State's economy and provides employment for their people.

State incentives vary from state to state and are normally designed to attract entrepreneurs based on the type of investment that is most beneficial to a particular state.

Examples of incentives by state governments:

- Assistance and guidance to entrepreneurs in setting up industrial units
- Enable entrepreneurs to get different industrial approvals and clearances from various departments and agencies from a single location.
- Register small industries, tiny industries, small-scale service and business enterprises.
- Sanction incentives to industrial units that are eligible.
- Help in locating land in the state for your Industrial setup.
- Provide marketing assistance to local industrial units.
- Rehabilitate sick small industrial units
- Exemption from sales taxes etc. for a period of time to help initial setup of the business.
- Help with loans, loan guarantees.
- Technology Parks where IT firms already have infrastructure available to start their business.
- Purchase commitment of some of your produced goods by the government.
- Help in exporting your products.

State governments in India naturally want new business to

setup in their state. Each state offers their own set of incentives to entrepreneurs. To find out the current incentives offered by various States, visit their websites. Links to some of the some state government websites are provided, to make it easier to find them. Readers can use the links provided to visit the state government website where they are considering a new venture and get up to date current information.

STATE	**WEBSITE ADDRESS**
Andhra Pradesh	http://www.aponline.gov.in/apportal/index.asp
Haryana	http://hsiidc.org.in/
Chhattisgarh	http://www.csidc.in/
Himachal Pradesh	http://hpsidc.nic.in/
Tripura	http://www.indiamart.com/tripura-industrial-development/
Goa	http://www.goaidc.com/coreinformation.html
Uttar Pradesh	http://upsidc.com/

100% Export Oriented Unit

Export Oriented Units (EOU) are 100% export units that can be set up anywhere in the country. The Government of India offers many incentives to EOU businesses as they earn valuable foreign exchange.

EOU advantage is that while they have a manufacturing unit in India, they are normally exempt from a lot of customs duty requirements that are placed on local manufacturing units. EOU units, basically operate as if they are not located inside India. The thinking here being that such units provide employment in India.

EOU units are supposed to export 100% of their produce. Even though they are restricted form selling in the domestic markets, they can sell up to 50% of the FOB value of exports in the domestic market on payment of duties.

Production and operation of 100 per cent EOU is setup in a customs bonded factory, unless specifically exempt from physical bonding; Goods will be imported into the customs bonded factory. EOU units are required to export its entire production, for a period of 10 years ordinarily and 5 years in case of products liable to rapid technological change.

EOU can normally be set up anywhere in the country, subject to environmental rules and regulations. They may be engaged in the manufacture and production of software, floriculture, horticulture, agriculture, aquaculture, animal husbandry, poultry and sericulture or other similar activities.

EOU is required to achieve the minimum Net Foreign Exchange

Earning (NFEP) as a percentage of exports and the minimum EP (Export Performance) as per the provisions of EXIM Policy which vary from sector to sector.

Incentives to EOU

- No import licenses are required by the EOU units and import of all industrial inputs exempt from customs duty.
- Supplies from the 'Domestic Tariff Area' to EOU are regarded as deemed exports and are hence exempt from payment of excise duty, which means that high quality inputs are available at lower costs.
- On fulfillment of certain conditions, EOU are exempted from payment of corporate income tax for a block of 5 years in the first 8 years of operation. Export earnings continue to be exempt from tax even after the tax holiday is over.
- Industrial plots and standard design factories are available to EOU at concessional rates.
- Single window clearance for EOU.

Software Technology Parks

Software Technology Parks of India (STPI) is a society set up by the Ministry of Communication and Information Technology, Government of India, with the objective of encouraging, promoting and boosting software exports from India.

The Software Technology Park scheme is a 100% export oriented scheme, for the development and export of computer software & services, using data communication links or in the form of physical media. The 100% Export Oriented Unit scheme

(STP scheme) is for setting up of software development and IT enabled services unit in India, for 100% Export. The STP scheme is administered by the Directors of STPI.

Benefits of STP Scheme

- 100% Customs duty exemption on imports
- Equipment can also be imported on loan or lease basis.
- All relevant equipment/goods including second hand equipment can be imported (except prohibited items)
- 100% excise duty exemption on local procurement.
- Central Sales Tax reimbursement on local purchases.
- Green card enabling priority treatment for Government clearances and other services.
- 100% foreign equity investment in the companies permissible under the 'Automatic Route' of RBI.
- Sales in the DTA (Domestic Tariff Area) up to 50% of the foreign exchange earned by the unit.

Procedure to become STP Member

To establish a STP Unit, register with STPI and become an STP member. The application form is available free of charge and can be downloaded from the STPI websites. Duly filled form along with applicable documents is required for membership.

The website link to Software Technology Parks of India (STPI) is: https://www.stpi.in/

Starting a new manufacturing unit in India

Those who are thinking about setting up a new manufacturing unit in India should realize that this is no easy task. The initial setting up of infrastructure alone can be costly and time consuming. Even to start a small factory, one needs to purchase or lease land, or perhaps a shed where the factory can be setup. Then they face the formidable task of trying to get the connections of various utilities, get the appropriate licenses etc. to get their new business up and running.

Before they know it, the costs of their project will skyrocket as they try to get through all the formalities of starting a manufacturing unit from scratch. There is an easier way! Purchase a sick unit.

What are Sick Units

Industrial units that are unable to financially sustain themselves are generally called 'sick units' in India. However, many sick units are not beyond redemption and can be revived, to become profitable.

Most sick units are factories that were operating businesses for some period of time, before being declared as sick units. A Sick unit usually will already have all the required licenses to operate, have machinery already setup and ready to go.

Some may wonder, why would a manufacturing unit be declared a sick unit? Normally, the main reason is that they are not financially viable. In other words they did not make a profit and owe money to financial institutions. Acquiring a sick manufacturing unit may be beneficial to new entrepreneurs.

Sick Industrial Units – A Goldmine for Investors

For smart entrepreneurs this could be goldmine in disguise. Let's consider a few obvious questions that arise on this topic. Why buy someone else's failed project? Let's look into the cause of why a particular manufacturing company, would be declared a sick unit and stop functioning.

There could be many reasons for this, if the product being produced, has gone out of style and is no longer valid, the answer is obvious. However, this is usually not the case with most sick units. Some of the reasons for which many of them end up as sick units are:

- Incompetent management
- Over-staffing
- Outdated production equipment and techniques
- Owners intentionally let their unit go sick!

To understand a bit more on this topic, let's consider how some industrial loans are approved.

How Loans for Industrial Ventures are given

Generally, loans are given to small industry by various financial institutions, based on collateral or government guarantees. Normally, a bank may expect a manufacturer to invest say, 25% of the cost of the project and provide a loan for the remaining 75%.

A promoter may get a project report prepared for suppose Rs five crore, and invest Rs 1.25 crore of his own money. The loan amount of Rs 3.75 crore is given to the promoter for his project. A dishonest promoter, could now control the money, and pad expenses to run the unit into being declared sick. Banks do have some extent of checks, but wherever human element is involved, sometimes just about everything can be overlooked and agreed upon.

Many sick units valued at several crore rupees are waiting for buyers. Sick units may have land, buildings, machinery, raw material and other assets. You've probably heard of banks in the west sometimes accepting ten cents to a dollar on loans, sick units with the right timing and approach can be such a deal for the smart investor.

Revive sick manufacturing unit

The choice of the authorities is always to make an effort to revive sick units, as this helps the Indian economy and the local population with employment. Genuine offers from entrepreneurs, to revive a sick unit may have a good chance of being approved. This is perhaps to easiest route to start a manufacturing unit in India.

Buying a Sick Industrial Unit

The Board for Industrial and Financial Reconstruction (BIFR) is the authority, which must approve takeover of a sick unit. NRIs who wish to get more information, about sick units' availability in a particular state, should contact the state industrial development authorities for information.

If starting a manufacturing unit in India is something that appeals to you. Then investing in a sick unit and restarting it, may be a route that may save you a lot of time and money.

Return to India planning

Relocating to India from abroad requires careful planning. NRIs who wish to return to India, should have a clear plan of what they intend to do after their return to India.

NRIs who return to India after a long absence have to go through a transition period, to get used to the Indian environment. If they can survive the initial transition period on their return to India, they will find that there are many positive sides to living in India.

Many people abroad of Indian origin may be planning a return to India, for various purposes. Non-resident professionals are also returning to India, perhaps with new business startups in mind. The reasons normally stated are, depressed economy in the west, greater advancement opportunities in India, superior schooling when compared to foreign schools and the desire to return home to family and friends.

Points worth considering before Returning to India

- Don't burn your bridges! While returning to India may be something you look forward to, things may not be what you expect when you do return to India. Have a backup plan just in case you decide to leave India again.
- Steps should be taken to declare non-residency in the country of your citizenship, so that you can minimize tax liabilities. Many countries tax their citizens on their worldwide income. Declaring yourself as a non-resident may help you minimize your taxes liability.

- Have a clear plan of what you will do in India. Have a business plan if you want to set up a business.
- Those who expect to look for employment in India? Should make an effort find a job before making a final move.
- Investigate housing, schools, and business opportunities etc. to some extent before making your move. The internet is the best medium to reach out anywhere, from the comfort of your home.

Planning date of return to save taxes in India

NRIs returning to India for settlement can save taxes and prolong their RNOR status by planning their date of arrival in India.

- Arriving in India after April 1st ensures that you were not present in the previous taxation year.
- Arriving in India after October 1st means you will be in India less than 183 days for that taxation year.

Status of Person after Return to India

NRIs when they return to India should be aware of the change in their status for tax purposes in India. Tax liability in India of a person returning to India, depends on the residential status of the person as per Indian Income tax Act 1961.

For the purpose of taxation, residential status in India has three classifications:

1. Resident and ordinarily resident (ROR)
2. Resident but NOT ordinarily resident.
3. Non Resident (NRI)

Returning non-residents, who have **NOT** been resident in India for nine years or more **or** if they have spent less than 729 days in India in the last 7 years, are deemed to be not ordinarily resident in India for taxation purposes. They are considered to have **RNOR** status. Those with **R**NOR status are taxed in India only on income derived in India. Their overseas income is exempt.

When the RNOR status of a returning resident expires, they are considered to be of resident status (ROR) and income earned overseas becomes taxable in India.

Persons of Indian origin, returning to India should be aware, that their foreign income may also be taxable as per laws of the country where they hold foreign assets. In most cases, relief from dual taxation is available in the form of a tax credit, for taxes paid to the other country because of Double Tax Avoidance Agreements (DTAA) that India has signed.

Assets held abroad - Points to consider:

- Foreign assets held by returning non-residents such as bank deposits, real estate, stocks, insurance policies etc. that were acquired before returning to India can continue to be held abroad. Such investments can continue to accrue income outside India.
- Returning NRIs can continue to hold their properties outside India. Such properties can be rented out or sold. Rental income or the sale proceeds can be credited to overseas bank accounts.
- In case s where a person returning to India for permanent residence, brings back foreign assets, they would be exempt from tax in India.
- Previously, assets acquired with money brought in to India by NRIs within one year after their return to India, was exempt from wealth taxes for a period of seven years after their return. However, this no longer applies. See update below:

UPDATE: Wealth Tax has been abolished in India from the financial year 2015-2016. An announcement to this effect was made by the Indian Finance Minister Mr. Arun Jaitley during the Budget 2015.

- Returning residents with RNOR status are not taxed on their foreign income in India. When their RNOR status expires they can still avail any tax relief available under Double Taxation Avoidance Agreement between India and the country from where their overseas income occurs in.

♦♦♦

Bank Accounts of NRIs returning to India

NRIs, who return to India for permanent residence, are expected to re-designate their non-resident bank accounts to local bank accounts. The choices available to them are as follows:

- NRO Accounts re-designated to ordinary resident account.
- NRE Account balances can be transferred to a Resident Foreign Currency (RFC) account. This is a resident foreign currency account that returning NRIs are permitted by RBI to open in India. RFC accounts can be maintained in foreign currencies such as USD, GBP, EUR and JPY.
- FCNR Account can be held until maturity and then re-designated to resident account or RFC account.

♦♦♦

Benefits of Resident Foreign Currency (RFC) accounts

- RFC accounts are fully repatriable.
- Those who receive a foreign pension can have their pension deposited in RFC accounts.
- Any foreign income or money transferred from abroad can be deposited in RFC accounts.
- Interest income on RFC deposits is not taxable as long as the returning resident has RNOR (resident not ordinarily resident) status. Once the person becomes an ordinary resident, interest income on this account becomes taxable.

Customs duty in India

All travelers arriving in India from abroad are required to comply with provisions of the Indian Customs Law. The owner of any baggage must for the purpose of clearing it, make a declaration of its contents to the customs officer and pay applicable customs duty, assessed by the customs authorities.

Tourists, normally have the facility to use the 'Green' or 'Red' channel of exit, depending on the goods they are importing into the country. Green channel exit, is for those who have nothing to declare to the customs authorities.

How customs duty is calculated in India

Basically there are two methods of applying customs duty.

1. Specific rate of duty
2. Ad-Valorem rate of duty

Specific rate of duty is based on the quantity of the item, such as size, weight etc. For example, 10 grams of gold would attract a certain specified amount of customs duty.

Ad-Valorem rate of duty is based on the value of the item and NOT on the weight.

Example: Several years ago, customs duty on gold taken to India by passengers was:

- Rs 300 per 10gm + 3% education cess on gold bars **other** than tola bars, bearing manufacturers or refiners engraved serial number and weight expressed in metric units and gold coins. [**Specific rate of duty**]

- As of January 17, 2012 the method of calculating customs duty on gold was changed to what is called the **Ad-Valorem rate of duty**. Instead of weight of the gold, the value of the gold is now used to assess customs duty.

Duty Free Allowances for Tourists

Duty Free Allowances of tourists are based on the incoming passenger's citizenship, country from where the tourist is coming from and whether they are of Indian origin.

Duty free allowances

The Baggage (Amendment) Rules, 2006 (Baggage Rule, 1998) currently apply to resident & non- resident Indians, who are returning to India. In the Union Budget 2014, Finance minister Mr. Jaitley announced an increase in customs duty exemptions for air travelers.

Duty free exemptions for adults:

- Indian passengers over the age of 10 years of age, returning from an overseas stay of more than 3 days are allowed to bring back used personal belongings except jewelry, without paying any duty.
- They can also bring back other assets within a limit of Rs.45, 000 as accompanied baggage.
- In case their stay is of three days or less, then the amount is reduced to Rs. 17,500.
- The free allowance cannot be pooled with the free allowance of any other passenger even if they are traveling together.

- One laptop computer (notebook computer) over and above the said free allowances mentioned above is also allowed duty free if imported by any passenger 18 years of age or above.
- Indian citizens, OCI holders as well as foreigners who normally reside in India and are returning from a visit abroad may carry Indian currency up to Rs. 25,000/- any amount over this needs to be declared.
- The goods over and above the free allowances are currently charged customs duty @ 35% + an education cess of 3% making the effective customs duty rate 36.05%. This rate does not apply for Alcoholic drinks and tobacco products imported in excess of allowed amounts. For these items the applicable commercial import rates are charged.

Duty free exemptions for children

- Indian passengers up to the age of 10 years of age, returning from an overseas stay of more than 3 days are allowed to bring back used personal belongings except jewelry, without paying any duty.
- They can also bring back other assets within a limit of Rs.17, 500 as accompanied baggage.
- In case their stay is of three days or less, then the amount is reduced to Rs. 3,000.

The following items are not allowed to be imported duty free and cannot be included in a person's duty free allowance.

- Firearms.
- Cartridges of fire arms exceeding 50

- Cigarettes exceeding 100 or cigars exceeding 25 or tobacco exceeding 125 grams.
- Alcoholic liquor or wines in excess of two liters
- Gold or silver, in any form, other than ornaments.
- Flat Panel (LCD/LED/Plasma) Television.

Additional duty free allowances

- Indian passengers returning from an overseas stay of at least 3 months are allowed to bring back used household belongings up to a maximum worth of Rs.12, 000, without paying any duty. They can also bring back other professional equipment within a limit of Rs.20, 000 as accompanied baggage. Professional equipment refers to portable instruments, gadgets and apparatus used by the passenger in his/her profession.
- In case the stay abroad is of at least 6 months, the professional equipment allowance limit is increased to Rs. 40,000 as accompanied baggage.
- Indian passengers returning from an overseas stay of at least 365 days during the last 2 years, and have not availed any concession on customs duty in the last 3 years, are allowed to bring back used personal and household effects up to a maximum worth of Rs.75, 000.
- In the case of Jewelry, male passengers who have lived abroad for more than a year, are entitled to bring back articles worth Rs.50, 000, female passengers are allowed up to Rs.100, 000.
- NRIs visiting India are allowed personal effects and other articles which they would be taking back with them, when they return abroad. Sometimes, customs officer will

endorse such items on the arriving passenger's passport to indicate the items that must be taken back when the passenger departs. In case the items that have to be taken back are not available when the passenger departs, they have to pay the applicable customs duty on those items.

Customs duty, on articles that exceed the duty free allowance are normally charged @ of 35%, plus an education cess of 3% (which works out to 36.05%)

Note: *Customs duty rates provided for general knowledge purposes and are subject to change by the authorities.*

For the latest information visit the official Indian Customs website: http://www.cbec.gov.in

Tourists of Foreign origin visiting India

Tourists of foreign origin <u>other than those of</u>

- Nepalese origin coming from Nepal **or**
- Of Bhutanese origin coming Bhutan **or**
- Of Pakistani origin coming from Pakistan.

Are allowed to bring in used personal effects and travel souvenirs, if -

- These goods are for personal use of the tourist, and these goods, other than those consumed during their stay in India, are re-exported when the tourist leaves India for a foreign destination.
- Articles up to a value of Rs.8000 for making gifts.

Tourists of Pakistani Origin duty free allowance

Pakistani origin tourists arriving by air are allowed to bring in their used personal effects, if these goods are for personal use of the tourist, and these goods, other than those consumed during the stay in India, are re-exported when the tourist leaves India for a foreign destination. They can also bring in articles up to a value of Rupees 6000 for making gifts.

Re-export option if unable to pay duty

In a situation where, one finds themselves charged with customs duty for items, and they are not in a position to pay the assessed duty. The arriving passenger may have an option to request the customs officer to detain their baggage (items on which customs duty is payable) either for re-export at the time of their departure from India or for clearance subsequently on payment of duty.

In such a case, the detained baggage would be examined, and full details of contents inventoried and kept in the custody of the customs department. A receipt is issued to the passenger.

Import of Gold by passenger

Any passenger of Indian Origin or a passenger holding a valid passport, issued under the Passport Act, 1967, who is coming to India after a period of not less than six months of stay abroad, can import gold as part of their baggage.

Short visits, if any, made by the passenger during the aforesaid period of six months may be ignored if the total duration of stay on such visits does not exceed thirty days.

Import of Gold by Non-Residents

A non-resident Indian can import gold in any form up to 1 Kgs. at a time, provided they are coming to India after 6 months stay abroad.

Kindly note the earlier limit of 10 Kgs has been reduced to 1 Kg by the Government of India with effect from April 18th 2012.
To view a copy of the government notification check http://nriinformation.com/faq1/index_htm_files/Gold_Press_Release_OneKg.pdf

Customs duty on gold taken to India

Currently the rate of customs duty charged in India on gold bars that show the serial number, weight and the manufacturer's name is 4%. All other type of gold, including jewelry items are charged duty @ 10%

How duty value of gold determined in India

The value of gold when it comes to calculation of customs duty in India, is determined by what is called the 'notified value'. This refers to a value that is determined by the Government of India from time to time.

Even though a passenger may have a receipt showing a value, the duty will be accessed by customs officers in India based on the 'notified value'. *(Rates provided subject to change by authorities)*

Conditions applicable to gold import as baggage

- The duty has to be paid in convertible foreign currency.

- The weight of gold (including ornaments) should not exceed 1 Kg per passenger. [the previous 10 Kg limit was reduced to 1 Kg by the Government of India with effect from April 18, 2012]
- The passenger should not have brought gold or other ornaments during any of his visits in the last six months i.e. he has not availed of the exemption under this scheme, at the time of short visits.
- Ornaments studded with stones and pearls are not allowed to be imported.
- The passenger can either bring the gold themselves at the time of arrival or import the same within fifteen days of their arrival in India as unaccompanied baggage.

Taking jewelry out of India by passenger

There is no value limit on the export of gold jewelry by a passenger as part of their baggage, so long as it constitutes the legal baggage of the passenger.

A passenger may request the Customs, for issue of an export certificate at the time of their departure from India, in respect of jewelry carried by them.

Export certificates are issued by the Customs authorities after they do a valuation of the gold being declared. The export certificate will show the person's details such as name, passport number and details of gold such as weight etc. Invoices or valuation appraisal from approved jewelers may be required to expedite the issue of export certificate.

Once an export certificate has been obtained, the items mentioned in the export certificate can be taken in or out of India without having to worry about customs duties.

Import of Silver

Non Resident Indians can import silver in any form up to 10 Kgs at a time, provided they are coming to India after 6 months stay abroad. Duty is payable @ 6% Ad-Valorem + 3% Education Cess. This customs duty must also be paid in foreign currency. Tariff value of silver is taken as per the notifications issued periodically by the authorities.

Import of Jewelry

A passenger who has been residing abroad for over 1 year and is returning to India, may be allowed to import duty free, jewelry up to a value of Rs.50,000/- in case of male passenger and Rs.100,000/- in case of female passenger. Import of jewelry in excess of this value will be charged customs duty.

Transfer of Residency – Customs duty

NRI/PIO who are returning to India for an extended period, have the option of availing the benefits under 'Transfer of Residency' and take advantage of relaxed customs duties under 'Transfer of Residency' (TR) rules.

Transfer of Residence is a facility provided to persons who intend to transfer their residence to India, after a stay abroad of at least two years. This facility allows the import of personal and household articles free of duty, and certain other listed items on payment of a concessional rate of duty. Even a car is allowed to be imported under TR rules, on payment of applicable customs duty.

Those taking transfer of residence are no longer subjected to any minimum stay requirements in India. They are free to leave India whenever they wish to. The only restriction is that they or their family members cannot avail TR benefits again for three years.

Transfer of Residence Rules (TR)

Requirements to qualify for transfer of residency concessions:

- A minimum stay of two years abroad, immediately preceding the date of arrival on transfer of residency is required.
- Total stay in India on short visits during the 2 preceding years should not exceed 6 months, and
- Passenger has not availed concessions under transfer of residency in the preceding three years.

Items allowed duty free

- Used personal articles
- household effects

Used personal articles

These would include used items required for day-to-day personal use, like all used items of personal wear such as, shirts, suits, shoes, wristwatch, saris, cosmetics in use, towels, toiletries, bedding, hearing aids, etc.

Household effects

Household effects comprise of items already in use in the household of the passenger, items such as, furniture, kitchen utensils, books, cassettes and CDs, wall clocks, fans, lights etc.

Value of goods allowed under TR rules

The total combined value of such goods should not exceed rupees five lakhs. NRIs should also be aware that not more than one unit, of each item of such goods is allowed, per family.

Items allowed duty free under transfer of residence

- Used personal and household articles
- Jewelry up to Rs. 50,000 by a gentleman passenger or Rs. 100,000 for a lady passenger.
- Jewelry taken out earlier by the passenger or by a member of his family from India. (Proof may be required)
- Video Cassette Recorder or Video Cassette Player or Video Television Receiver or Video Cassette Disk Player.

- Washing Machine.
- Electrical or Liquefied Petroleum Gas Cooking Range
- Personal Computer(Desktop Computer)
- Laptop Computer(Notebook Computer)
- Domestic Refrigerators of capacity up to 300 liters or its equivalent.

List of items with reduced customs duty

For the following items a reduced customs duty of 15% plus a 3% educational cess is charged. It does not matter whether these items are new or old.

- Television
- Digital Video Disc Player.
- Video Home Theatre System.
- Dish Washer.
- Music System.
- Air Conditioner.
- Domestic refrigerators of capacity above 300 liters or its equivalent.
- Deep Freezer.
- Microwave Oven.
- Video camera or the combination of any such video camera with one or more of the following goods, namely:-
  (a)Television Receiver;
  (b)Sound recording or reproducing apparatus;
  (c)Video reproducing apparatus.
- Word Processing Machine.
- Fax Machine.

- Portable Photocopying Machine.
- Cinematographic films of 35 mm and above.

Leaving India after Transfer of Residence

A person, who had availed of concessions on transfer of his residence, can now leave the country without the permission of the Assistant Commissioner/Additional Commissioner of Customs. However, such a person will not be allowed to avail transfer of residence concession, for three years from the date that they had availed customs duty concessions under transfer of residency earlier.

Note: *Transfer of Residence concessions is available to a family as a whole. Individual members of the same family cannot claim separate concessions. Only one member of the family can claim such concessions*

Presence required during customs clearance

The person taking transfer of residency is usually required to be present during customs clearance. This is to answer any questions that the customs officer may have, regarding the ownership or usage of a particular item, being imported. Customs authorities may also require the importer to sign certain forms, in the presence of the customs officer. They also examine the goods in the presence of the importer.

Under exceptional cases, goods may be cleared without your personal presence, if you authorize someone to act on your behalf by way of a power of attorney and certain customs forms, are duly notarized or attested by a Gazetted officer of the Customs or Central Excise dept. However, this type of permission depends on Custom authorities.

Tip: Hire a customs broker, they may save you time & money.

Calculation of customs duty on baggage items

Normally, items that are imported as baggage and are over and above the duty exempt limit, are subjected to a uniform rate of customs duty, for ease of assessment.

When it comes to baggage of a passenger, there is no specific duty per item, the total value is taken into consideration and duty is charged, on the amount that is over the duty free allowance.

Example:

A passenger arrives with baggage that has duty payable items valued at suppose Rupees 45,000, and duty free allowance applicable to this passenger is Rupees 25,000. In such a scenario, customs duty would be charged on the total value of the goods less the duty free allowance. Rs. 45,000 – 25,000 so duty would be charged on Rs. 20,000

Calculating Customs Duty on used items

In case a person knows the rate of duty for a particular item, it's easy to calculate the duty that will be charged. However for used items the value is determined by allowing depreciation on a yearly basis. Normally depreciation would be calculated as:

- First year depreciation @ 16%
- Second year depreciation @ 12%
- Third year depreciation @ 10%

Automobile imports

The following persons are entitled for car import in India for noncommercial use, on payment of stipulated customs duty.

- Individuals coming to India on 'Transfer of Residence' for permanent settlement after two year's continuous stay abroad.
- Resident Indians, gifted with a car as an award in any international event/match/competition.
- Legal heirs/successors of deceased relatives residing abroad.
- Physically disabled persons. *(See conditions that apply at the end of this chapter)*
- Companies incorporated in India having foreign equity participation.
- Branches/offices of foreign firms.
- Charitable/missionary institutions registered with the Ministry of Welfare and the Ministry of Home Affairs, Government of India.
- Honorary Consuls of Foreign Countries on the recommendations of the Ministry of External Affairs, Government of India.
- Journalists/Correspondents of foreign news agencies, having accreditation certificate with the Press Information Bureau, Ministry of Broadcasting in India.

Car Imports on Transfer of Residence by NRI

Cars can be imported to India only by those NRIs who are transferring residence to India from abroad. In such a case, the engine capacity of the car should be less than 1600cc for new cars. This limit does not apply to secondhand cars. Used car being brought in on transfer of residency, should have been:

- In the owner's possession, for at least one year abroad.
- Proof of one year old registration, in the owner's name may be required by the customs authorities in India.

Rules for NRI car imports

The restrictions imposed and conditions placed on import of cars for commercial purposes, do not apply in the case of passengers bringing their own used car on 'Transfer of Residency'. While NRIs do not require an import license, to take their car to India, the following conditions apply:

Car import to India under Transfer of Residency

- The person importing the automobile should have been abroad continuously for a period of not less than two years.
- The vehicle should be imported into India within six months of arrival in India.
- The purchase consideration for the car should have been made abroad.
- The car should have been in use, for a minimum of one year, before the importer's return to India.
- Customs duty that is applicable in India can be paid by funds

remitted from abroad, or by debit to the importers NRE/FCNR/RFC account.

- Where a handicapped person is concerned, the import duty can be paid in Indian currency. Government's permission is required before such cars can be sold.
- There should not be a time gap of more than six months, between the importer's arrival in India and the import of the car.
- NRIs importing cars under transfer of residency, can sell the vehicle anytime in India after it has been legally imported.
- A license is required for the import of spares.
- The market price would be the basis at which the import duty would be calculated. While the trade discount and depreciation, on the value are deducted from the price, freight from the country of manufacture and insurance charges, are added on to it, in addition to the landing charges.
- There should be a time gap of five years before the importer can import another car. This applies in cases where a person leaves India and subsequently returns to India again, under transfer of residence.

Customs authorities usually will endorse on the passport of the importer "Transfer of residence with car" at the time of clearance of the car.

Documents for customs clearance of cars

- Owner's original passport.
- Original overseas registration certificate of the vehicle.
- Original manufacturers/suppliers invoice.
- Current insurance policy of the vehicle.
- List of car accessories along with make and model number.
- Original bill of lading.

Cost, Insurance and Freight (CIF) value of imported cars should be calculated for customs duty. Cost in case of new vehicles is the transaction value between the seller and the buyer. In case of old and used vehicles, the cost is calculated by taking the value of the vehicle in the year of manufacture, after allowing depreciation.

Depreciation Percentage on Used Cars Maximum Deprecation Allowed is 70%	
Period of Usage	**Depreciation**
For every quarter during 1st year	4%
For every quarter during 2nd year	3%
For every quarter during 3rd year	2.5%
For every quarter during 4th year	2%

Calculating custom duty on car's

India has 100 percent customs duty on all car imports irrespective of their engine capacity and brand. There are also other taxes added on such as VAT, Excise duty, CVD etc. The total Customs duty incidence on cars comes to around 181%

Car Import guidelines

Individuals who are eligible to import a vehicle can import one car; companies with foreign equity participation and branches/offices of foreign firms can import a maximum of three vehicles.

Physically disabled persons can import, only specially designed vehicles suitable for use by disabled. Vehicles imported for physically disabled persons are not eligible to be sold for two years. The 'No Sale' condition for 2 years is endorsed by the Customs Authorities on the passport/registration documents at the time of import and also by the Regional Transport Authorities (RTO), when such vehicles are presented for registration in India.

All such car imports, except those done by the physically disabled persons, should not involve any foreign exchange remittance from India directly or indirectly.

Importing Cars for physically handicapped Persons

Import of cars specially designed for the physically handicapped are allowed. Such imports are permitted on the basis of a certificate, from the State Civil Surgeon or Head of the concerned wing in the Government Hospital.

The certificate should clearly certify, that the importer has any of the following disabilities:

- Unilateral/Bilateral amputees of the lower limbs excluding below knee unilateral.
- Unilateral below elbow or above elbow ambuacee.
- Traumatic/permanent paralysis which cannot be surgically or medically treated.
- Permanent paralysis of one upper limbs or lower limbs due to any reason or hemipares.
- Grossly deformed limbs due to trauma arthritis or congenital but having at least one upper limb normal.

Certificate must verify that the percentage of impairment is not less than 50% of the total body, as per Mebride Scale:

Other conditions

1. If the car is a gift, confirmatory letter from donor, in original, which should also indicate the donor's relationship with the donee.
2. Satisfactory evidence, clearly justifying the need and essentiality for import of a self-driven car by the applicant.
3. Import of only one car up to 1600 CC engine capacity is allowed.
4. Car shall not be allowed to be sold or possession parted with, or pledged, mortgaged or hypothecated at any time. However, in special circumstances, and for valid reasons, and subject to such conditions as may be laid down, the

Director General of Foreign Trade, New Delhi may on request, relax this condition.

5. The importer shall produce his driving license within 6 months from the date of import, to the licensing authority with whom 'No Sale Bond' is executed.
6. The Customs duty may be paid in Indian rupees.

Firearm import

Persons bringing their effects on transfer of residency, can bring one firearm of permissible bore on payment of applicable customs duty, subject to the conditions that:-

(a) The firearm was in possession and in use by them abroad for a minimum period of one year.
(b) The passenger has a valid arms license from the local Indian authorities.
(c) Subject to the condition that such firearm, after clearance, shall not be sold, loaned, transferred or otherwise parted with, for consideration or otherwise, during the lifetime of the person importing the firearm.
(d) Customs duty @153% ad-valorem [subject to change]

How to apply for Fresh Arms License?

The applications for the grant of Arm Licenses are submitted in the office of District Commissioner of Police/Licensing by applicants. Forms are available at the reception desk of the DCP.

The following documents are required to be submitted with application form:-

- ✓ Application on the prescribed Performa "A" (available at Reception in DCP Licensing office)
- ✓ Four passport size photographs. One photo is attached on the form, the other three duly attested, on the reverse by a Gazetted officer to be submitted along with the form.
- ✓ Attested copy of the proof of residence such as: Ration Card, Voter Identity Card, Passport, Electricity Bill etc.

✓ Posting certificate/recommendation from the Commanding Officer (in case of Armed Force personnel).

Renewal of Firearm License

Licenses are normally issued for three years. To renew arm license, a license renewal application is made on the prescribed form. The steps for renewal of license involve:

- Documents Verification
- Submission of renewal application form duly filled, along with required documents of proof of residence.
- Inspection of your weapon for which the license is being renewed.
- Criminal Antecedent's Check. This is a process, where the particulars of the licensee are checked, with the crime record office database, to ascertain if there has been any involvement of the licensee, in a criminal offence.
- Fee payment for renewal
- Renewal of license and its endorsement in the copy of the license.

License Renewal Time

The licensee can apply for renewal of their license, from one month in advance to one month later from the date of expiry of license. This period is treated as valid period for renewal and within this period, only the due fees are be charged.

Right to Information Act (RTI)

The Right to Information Act (RTI) was passed by Parliament on 15 June 2005 and came fully into force on October 13, 2005.

The purpose of the RTI act is to provide transparency and accountability in the working of every public authority. It gives Indian citizens the right to information that is under the control of various public authorities such as government offices, municipal offices, hospitals and public sector companies.

All websites of the government of India have a link to their RTI pages. These pages provide information of the personnel to whom RTI related requests can be sent to.

RTI for Non-Residents

NRIs and persons of Indian origin are also allowed to use India's Right to Information Act. RTI has helped many people get information from various government offices and resolve issues.

Right to Information includes the right to:

1. Inspect works, documents and records.
2. Take notes, extracts or certified copies of documents or records.
3. Take certified samples of material.
4. Obtain information in form of printouts, diskettes, floppies, tapes, video and cassettes or in any other electronic mode.

Furthermore, under Section 4(1) (d), an applicant can ask for "reasons" behind an administrative or quasi-judicial decision of a public authority, especially if she/he is an "affected person".

RTI - Public Information Officers

Authorities have appointed public information officers (PIO), both for the central government (CPIO's) as well as the state governments (SPIO's) and they are responsible, to give information to a person who seeks information under the RTI Act.

Assistant Public Information Officer (APIO)

APIO are officers at the sub-divisional level, to whom a person can give his RTI application or appeal. The APIO will send the applications or appeals to the appropriate PIO.

The Department of Posts has appointed APIO, for all the public authorities under the Government of India, in various post offices across India. Chances are you may be able to submit your RTI application, to a post office in most Indian cities.

How to submit RTI application

RTI applications can be submitted by writing preferably on a white sheet of paper. Your application should include:

- Your name, address, contact telephone number and your email ID.
- Information about Public Information officer, name, address etc. *(Normally shown on the concerned departments websites on their RTI page)*
- Confirmation of payment of fee.

In case you have problems locating your PIO/APIO, you can address your RTI application to the PIO C/o Head of Department and send it to the concerned Public Authority with the requisite application fee.

The Head of Department will have to forward your application to the concerned PIO. It is recommended, that you not address your RTI application to the PIO by their name. This is a precaution, just in case the person gets transferred or a new PIO is designated in their place.

RTI Fee

Generally fee can be paid in person or by demand draft, Indian postal order etc. Fee for RTI has been kept to a minimum level so as to be affordable to all. For Central Departments a fee of Rupees 10 is charged for filing RTI application.

There are other small charges, for photo copy etc. when requesting information. A charge of Rupees 2 per page is levied for information provided. There is also a charge of Rupees 5 for each hour of inspection after the first hour. All fees are subject to change. The fee structure mentioned above is for the Central Government in India, State Governments may have their own fee structure.

Most Government department websites have a link to their RTI page; this page should provide information about required fee and procedure to seek information from their offices.

Time limit for Response under RTI

The time limit for getting a response to your RTI inquiry, from the concerned Public Information Officer (PIO) is generally 30 days from the date your application is submitted.

In a case where the application is submitted to the Assistant PIO, five additional days are allowed. This is to provide for the required time for the APIO to send the application to the PIO. Taking all factors into account, one should expect a response with a time frame of approximately 40 days at the most.

Deemed Refusal

Failure to provide information within the specified period is deemed to be refusal to give you the information you requested. In such cases, you can go to the next RTI step of getting information, by way of an appeal.

Recourse in case of refusal

There may be cases where a Public Information Officer (PIO) may not act as per provisions of the Act, or an applicant may not be satisfied with the response of the Public Information Officer. The RTI act allows two appeals to deal with such situations.

- The first appeal is made to the First Appellate Authority (FAA) who is an officer of a senior rank, than the Public Information Officer, who initially handled your RTI application.
- First appeal has to be filed within 30 days, from date of receipt of decision of Central Public Information Officer by the applicant.
- In cases of deemed refusal, where no reply has been received, first appeal should be filed within 30 days (35 days if application is lodged with ACPIO) from the date of receipt by Central Public Information Officer (ACPIO)

Procedure for first appeal

To file the first appeal, you need to find the name, designation and address of the first appellate authority. This should be available on the response letter you receive for your RTI application.

In case no response has been received, visit the web-site of the concerned government department and refer to the RTI icon on their website homepage. Click the RTI icon and you should find the details of RTI contact names on their RTI pages.

In case despite your efforts you are unable to locate the details of the First Appeal Authority (FAA) you can address your first appeal as follows:

The First Appellate Authority under RTI Act 2005
C/O.
Head of ________________Dept. /office

You should also mention address of concerned PIO dept. /office.

RTI – Points to remember

- You can normally write the appeal on a plain white sheet of paper. Some state governments may have specified forms and this can be ascertained, from the appropriate government websites.
- Those who want to be present during the first appeal hearing, should mention this at the end of their appeal request.
- There is no fee prescribed for first appeal for Public

Authorities, under the Central Government.

- Some States have a prescribed fee and a specified format for First Appeal. If your First Appeal is to a Public Authority falling under State Government, applicants should check RTI Rules of individual States regarding First Appeal fees, mode of payment and the format of appeal requirement
- All photocopies of enclosures, mentioned in the appeal should be self-attested by the applicant under the word 'Attested' and with full signature.
- Applicants should always retain a copy of appeal and postal receipt. Send your application by registered post with an Acknowledgement Due card. Save the receipt as proof of mailing.
- First Appellate Authority (FAA) has to decide on the appeal within 30 days, from the date of receipt of first appeal. She/he can take a further 15 days (total 45 days), provided they give the reasons for the delay in writing.

RTI - Second Appeal

If the appellate authority (FAA) fails to pass an order on the appeal, within the prescribed period, or if the petitioner is not satisfied with the order of the first appellate authority. They have the option to file a second appeal with the Central Information Commission.

The second appeal must be within ninety days from the date on which the decision should have been made by the first appellate authority, or was actually received by the appellant.

The appeal made to the Central Information Commission (CIC) should contain the following information:

- Name and address of the appellant.
- Name and address of the Public Information Officer, whose decision is being appealed.
- Particulars of the order including number, if any, against which the appeal is preferred.
- Brief facts leading to the appeal.
- If the appeal is preferred against deemed refusal, particulars of the application including number and date and name and address of the Public Information Officer, to whom the application was made and relief sought.
- Grounds for the relief sought.
- Any other information that you think will help the Commission in deciding the appeal.

The appeal made to the Informational Commission should be accompanied by the following documents:

- Self-attested copies of the order or documents against which appeal is made.
- Copies of the documents relied upon by the appellant and referred to in the appeal.
- An index of the documents referred to in the appeal.

RTI is a great tool for the average citizen, they no longer need to pay bribes in offices to get information that they need.

RTI has been successfully used in India by many people to get issues resolved.

Whether your pension is being held back or the ration card application has received no response, RTI could be the key to get results in a fast and timely manner.

Exit Visa from India

Foreign nationals visiting India for pleasure normally do not require an exit visa to leave India provided; they entered India with a valid visa and leave India before their visas expire.

Exit Visa Requirement

An exit visa may normally be required in cases where:

- Passport with a valid visa stamped on it has been lost.
- Person's visa has expired and they have not left India
- New born baby in India. When someone visiting India from abroad, gives birth in India.

At the time of departure from India, documents are examined by the immigration authorities and in cases where visa has expired, permission to leave India may be denied by the authorities. In such a case, the traveler would be required to get an exit visa, before they are allowed to leave India legally.

To get an 'Exit Visa' in India, go to the local FRRO office and apply. A fee is charged for this and may vary depending on the country you are from.

Exit Visa when passport lost or stolen

In the unfortunate event where a passport is lost, there is a requirement that the loss must be reported to the local police and a copy of the police report obtained. The following documents are normally required to get an exit visa from the FRRO:

- Copy of Police report regarding the lost passport.

- Letter from concerned Embassy with details of lost passport and visa details.
- New Passport/Travel Document/Emergency Travel Certificate that may be issued by the concerned embassy.

The person who has lost their passport, would have to contact their embassy and get a new passport or travel document before the FRRO can issue an exit visa.

Keeping photo copies of travel documents

Keeping a photo copy of your passport and the page where your Indian visa is stamped is always advisable. In case of loss of passport, such photo copies provide your passport number and entry visa number to the authorities, and this should make it easier to get new documents issued.

Exit Visa for new born child

FRRO can issue exit visas to persons who have a valid, legal record of entry into India. However, FRRO offices do not have the authority to issue a visa to enter India. Only Indian consulates abroad have the authority to issue visas to enter India.

In a case where a child is born in India, there is no prior visa entry record. Hence FRRO cannot issue an exit visa for the child to leave India, unless they receive authorization from the Ministry of Home Affairs. Parents of new born children, for the issue of the first visa for their new born child, should approach the Ministry of Home Affairs, Foreign Division, Jaisalmer House, 26, Man Singh Road New Delhi.

Documents that are normally required by the Ministry of Home Affairs are the parent's passport and visa details, as well as the child's birth certificate.

After reviewing the required documentation, the Ministry of Home Affairs generally gives permission to the FRRO to issue the visa.

This authorization to the FRRO is normally, in a sealed letter given to the parents, who can take it to the concerned FRRO, pay the required fee and get the exit visa for their child.

Foreign exchange allowance

When I moved overseas in 1970, the Government of India allowed foreign exchange purchase of only US$ 8 when leaving India. Fortunately, India now has no shortage of foreign exchange and rules have changed considerably.

Tourists travelling abroad from India now, can take up to US$ 10,000 per year. Foreign exchange up to US$10,000, in any one calendar year may be obtained from any authorized dealer for tourism purposes. No RBI permission is required.

The stipulated ceiling of US$10,000 is applicable in aggregate and foreign exchange may be obtained for one or more than one visit, provided the aggregate foreign exchange availed of in one calendar year does not exceed the prescribed ceiling of US$10,000.

Note: No foreign exchange is available for visit to Nepal and/or Bhutan for any purpose.

Taking Indian currency in/out of India

Effective 19 June, 2014. The Reserve Bank of India (RBI) has allowed all residents and non-residents (except citizens of Pakistan and Bangladesh and also other travelers coming from and going to Pakistan and Bangladesh) to take out Indian currency notes while leaving the country.

- Residents and non-residents, except individuals from Pakistan and Bangladesh, can carry Indian currency up to Rs.25, 000 while leaving the country.
- They can also bring Indian currency up to Rs.25, 000 into India when they visit.

Frequently asked questions on Foreign Exchange

Q. Where can I exchange my Indian Rupees to US dollars?
A. Any authorized bank or authorized money changers. Money changers normally offer a slightly favorable exchange rate.

Q. Can I pay for the purchase of foreign exchange, by way of cash in India Rupees?
A. If the exchange you are purchasing is up to Rupees 50,000, cash payment in Indian Rupees can be made. However, in cases where the purchase amount will exceed Rupees 50,000, then the entire amount will have to be paid by way of a cheque (crossed, not bearer cheque) or bank draft.

Take Cash or Travelers Cheque?

When purchasing foreign currency in India, travelers are allowed to take up to US$ 2000 in cash and the rest has to be taken in the form of either traveler's cheque or a bank draft.

Up to US$ 5000 or its equivalent in cash is allowed for travelers going to:

- Iraq
- Libya

Up to US$ 10,000 or its equivalent in cash is allowed for travelers going to:

- Islamic Republic of Iran
- Russian Federation
- Other Republics of Commonwealth of Independent States

Q. I am going to UK for a business trip to promote my business. How much exchange can I get?

A. Authorized dealers are permitted to release foreign exchange equivalent to a maximum of US$ 25,000 for a business trip. If you need more then RBI permission is required.

Q. I am going to Nepal for a business trip. How much foreign exchange can I get?

A. You can't get any foreign exchange for trips to Nepal.

Q. I am planning to go abroad for study. How much foreign exchange can I get?

A. For each academic year, authorized dealers are allowed to release up to US$ 100,000. However, if more is required, then you need an estimate of the amount required from the education institute you are joining.

Students can also receive from relatives up to US$ 100,000 to help them meet their monetary requirements, while studying abroad.

Q. I have some Indian Rupees with me from my previous trip to India. Can I take this money back to India on my next trip legally?

A. Legally, up to Rupees 25,000 can be brought in from any country other than Pakistan and Bangladesh.

Q. How much cash in Indian currency can be taken out of India?

A. Export of Indian Currency has been relaxed. Currently Residents and non-residents, except individuals from Pakistan and Bangladesh, can carry Indian currency up to Rs.25, 000 while leaving the country.

Q. How much foreign exchange can I get for a tourism trip abroad without RBI permission?

A. Up to US$ 10,000 is allowed per financial year without RBI approval from authorized dealers. This does not apply if you are travelling to Nepal or Bhutan as no foreign exchange is given for these countries.

Q. I need to show a lump sum of money in my account to get immigration in Canada. How much money can I send from India for this purpose?

A. None! No amount of foreign exchange is allowed to be remitted outside India for the purpose of earning points for immigration visas.

Q. I have a job offered to me abroad, how much foreign exchange; will I be allowed to take?

A. Those going abroad for employment purposes are allowed up to US$ 100,000.

Q. How much foreign currency is allowed for study abroad?

A. Up to US$ 100,000 is allowed per academic year for those wanting to study abroad. If more money is required, then there is a requirement that an estimate from the university/college is required.

Q. What is the limit for medical treatment funds required abroad?

A. Those traveling out of India for medical treatment can get foreign exchange of US$ 100,000 based on a self-declaration. More money is allowed subject to getting an estimate from a doctor or hospital.

Insurance policies of NRIs

NRIs can continue to hold insurance policies they held abroad before moving back to India. No specific permission is required to hold such insurance policies.

*As per Reserve Bank Notification No. FERA.118/92-RB dated 7th September 1992:

**Persons who have returned to India after being a non-resident for a minimum continuous stay of one year abroad have been granted exemption from the requirement of obtaining permission of Reserve Bank for holding any life insurance policies taken out of foreign exchange lawfully acquired by them while they were resident outside India.*

They would also be free to retain the maturity proceeds or any claim amounts received on such policies in their foreign currency accounts in India (RFC accounts) or abroad.

Remittance of Premiums on Foreign Currency Policies

Persons, who are permanently resident in India, are not permitted to take life insurance policies with foreign insurance companies.

In cases where, foreign currency life insurance policies were taken out from foreign insurance companies, by persons while they were resident outside India and have returned to India for permanent residence, premiums due on such policies can be paid by them out of their entitlements under the Returning Indians Foreign Exchange Entitlement Scheme (RIFEE Scheme) or out of funds held in their foreign currency accounts abroad or in India (RFC accounts).

Remittances from India will, however, be allowed provided

(a) The policy had been in force for at least three years prior to policy holder's return to India; and

(b) An undertaking has been furnished by the policy holder to repatriate to India the maturity proceeds or any claim amounts due on the policy through an authorized dealer.

Schools in India

One of the questions that concern NRI parents who are contemplating a move back to India, is schooling of their children. When it comes to education, India has some great schools.

Children who move abroad with their parents from India, quite often do very well in western schools, as the schooling level in India when compared to schools in some foreign countries for subjects such as mathematics and science, is said to be much better.

Most NRI parents seeking admissions for their children, probably wonder about the syllabuses of Indian schools and the similarity if any, with western schools. Many schools in India now have adopted syllabuses that conform to internationally acceptable standards.

Schools in India are either municipal schools that are affiliated with the state governments or private schools. Regardless of whether they are municipal or private schools, each school is affiliated with one of the following:

1. State Secondary School Certificate (SSC) board
2. Council for the Indian School Certificate Examination (ICSE)
3. Central Board of Secondary Education (CBSE) boards.
4. International General Certificate of Secondary Education (IGCSE)
5. International Baccalaureate (IB)

Usually, a child in India, before joining the first standard, would attend a nursery school, pre-primary school or some sort of

Montessori school for about three years. The actual schooling would start at age five.

Stages of School Education in India

The Primary Stage consists of Classes I-V, i.e., of five year duration. The next stage of education can be characterized as the 'Middle Stage'. This would compromise of children studying in class six to eight. Next is the 'Secondary Stage' which leads up to grade nine to eleven and finally the board examinations.

Following completion of their secondary school education, students head to college. Typically in India, high school is considered to be grade 10 and Intermediate is grade 12. One may periodically hear 10 plus 2 in India.

♦♦♦

School Syllabus in India

A brief summary of the various school syllabus offered in India are provide below:

Secondary School Certificate (SSC)

This is provided by various Indian states such as, Gujarat, Andhra Pradesh, Maharashtra, Madhya Pradesh and Goa. SSC is quite popular in the state of Maharashtra.

The syllabus would depend on the state where the school is located. Normally the state syllabuses are considered to be easier than the other syllabuses in India, such as CBSE and ICSE. Some parents, in an effort to help their children get a higher mark in high school, switch them to the State syllabus from ICSE/CBSE.

Central Board of Secondary Education (CBSE)

They prepare the syllabus from KG to Class 12 for schools affiliated to them and have same syllabus throughout India. Their exams are also conducted at the same time all over India. CBSE has a national curriculum; this helps parents who move to different parts of India due to transfers etc.

Their children will follow the same syllabus if they join another CBSE affiliated school, regardless of the city or state they move to within India.

The majority of Indian competitive examinations such as, the All Indian Pre-Medical/Pre-Dental exams are based on CBSE syllabus.

Indian Certificate of Secondary Education (ICSE)

The ICSE board was formed in India in 1986. Many educational institutes follow their curriculum. Students prepare for All India Secondary School Examination for class 10 and the All India Senior Examination for class 12.

ICSE is Indian Certificate of Secondary Education, while the syllabus may have an international touch; it is primarily used in India.

International General Certificate Sec. Ed. (IGCSE)

Is a globally recognized qualification, The IGCSE curriculum has worldwide acceptance and credibility. It is recognized by colleges and universities in the commonwealth countries.

Schools in India with an international outlook, normally offer IGCSE.

IGCSE is a two-year programme starting at the Class 9 level. Students who have done their early schooling from any other board, can join the IGCSE programme up to the Class 9 level.

A student who has passed IGCSE is eligible for any +2 level qualifications, like Class 12 CBSE/ ICSE or any international pre-university programme, like the International Baccalaureate Diploma Programme (IBDP), Advanced Placement Diploma (US), and A/AS Level & Cambridge Advanced International Certificate of Education (AICE) UK.

International Baccalaureate (IB)

The IB programme was founded in 1968 by the International Baccalaureate Organization (IBO), a non-profit educational organization based in Geneva, Switzerland. The International Baccalaureate (IB) offers high quality programs of international education to a worldwide community of schools.

IB Diploma is recognized by schools and colleges at an international level.

There are three programs for students aged 3 to 19.

- The Primary Years Program (Kindergarten to Class 5).
- The Middle Years Program (Class 6 to Class 10).
- The Diploma Program (Class 11 to Class 12).

Schools recognized by the International Baccalaureate Organization and offering the IB curriculum are known as IB World Schools.

There are several schools in India that offer IB Diploma such as, American Embassy School, New Delhi and Canadian International School in Bengaluru, Karnataka. As I write this there are currently 84 schools in India, considered as IB World Schools.

Selecting a school in India

When it comes to selecting a school for their children, all Indian parents want their children to get the best education possible. Finding the right school of course is easier said than done. What might suit one child, may not be the ideal school for another. While searching for an appropriate school, keep in mind that a school that charges higher fee, does not necessarily make it more efficient than other schools.

Here are some recommendations on selecting a school that you may want to consider:

- If you have a syllabus in mind that you want your child to follow such as, CBSE, ICSE or IGCSE, then do a search only for schools that offer this curriculum. Once you find the schools offering your desired syllabus you can pay attention to the school that suits you most.
- School location will naturally play a part in your selection, unless you are seeking a boarding school for your child.
- Boarding schools in India are quite popular and many young children aged 6 years and up, go to boarding schools. Depending on how long your child has stayed away from India, it might be better to start them off in day school before opting for a boarding school.

- Schooling is a big business in India. School fees in India can be expensive, depending on the school selected. Some schools are quoting fees of Rupees 3 lakh to 6.5 lakh per year for children studying in junior classes.
- When visiting schools, inquire about student teacher ratio, teachers qualifications and background.

List of Schools in India

A list of 101 schools in India is provided in this book, along with their telephone numbers and website addresses. Schools are listed by city.

There are many other schools in India that have not been listed because listing every school is beyond the scope of this book. The list of schools provided here, is not intended to offer an opinion on any school.

Please note:

- As this book is intended for NRIs, I have tried, where ever possible, to include schools that offer an internationally accepted syllabus.
- Any school that does not have a workable website has not been listed. The reason for this is, that parents living abroad can easily find information about a school by visiting their websites. Most school websites should offer information such as admission procedures, school syllabus, fees etc.
- Parents should make it a point to visit schools in person to check out facilities rather than accepting what a schools website may state.
- Schools listed show their city, website link and contact telephone numbers.

Schools in Ahmedabad

1	**School**	Mahatma Gandhi International School
	Web:	http://www.idealfoundation.com/
	Tel:	91 79 646 3888

Schools in Badhani

2	**School**	Dalhousie Public School,
	Web:	http://www.dpsbadhani.com/school.html
	Tel:	91-186-3292233

Schools in Bengaluru

3	**School**	Bangalore International School
	Web:	http://www.bangaloreinternationalschool.com
	Tel:	91 80 284 45852
4	**School**	Canadian International School,
	Website	www.canadianinternationalschool.com
	Tel:	91 8042494444
5	**School**	Greenwood High
	Website	http://www.greenwoodhigh.edu.in
	Tel:	91 80 27802656
6	**School**	Indus International School
	Website	http://www.indusschool.com
	Tel:	91 080 2289 5990
7	**School**	Jain International Residential School

	Website	http://www.jirs.ac.in/
	Tel:	91 80 2757 7013
8	**School**	Sarala Birla Academy
	Website	http://saralabirlaacademy.com/
	Tel:	91 80 41348200
9	**School**	Stonehill International School
	Website	http://www.stonehillinternationalschool.org/
	Tel:	91 8043418300
10	**School**	The International School Bangalore
	Website	http://tisb.org/
	Tel:	91 8022 634900

Schools in Bhopal

11	**School**	Eastern Public School
	Website	http://www.e-p-s.in/
	Tel:	91 755 2805695

Schools in Bhubaneswar

12	**School**	KiiT International School
	Website	http://www.kiit-is.org/
	Tel:	91 9937220252

Schools in Chandigarh

13	**School**	Kundan International School

	Website	http://kundaninternational.org/
	Tel:	91 172 6531002
14	**School**	St. Xavier's Schools
	Website	http://www.stxaviers.com/index.asp
	Tel:	91-172-2607079
		Schools in Chennai
15	**School**	American International School
	Website	http://www.aisch.org/
	Tel:	91 44 2254 9000
16	**School**	M.Ct.M.Chidambaram Chettyar International
	Website	http://www.mctmib.org/
	Tel:	91 44 24992962
		Schools in Coimbatore
17	**School**	Chinmaya International Residential School
	Website	http://www.cirschool.org/
	Tel:	91 422 2613308
		Schools in Dalhousie
18	**School**	Guru Nanak Public School
	Website	http://gnpsdalhousie.com/index.htm
	Tel:	91-1899 240653
		Schools in Dehradun
19	**School**	SelaQui World School

	Website	http://www.selaqui.org/,
	Tel:	91 135 305 1009
20	**School**	The Doon School
	Website	http://www.doonschool.com/
	Tel:	91 135 2526 540
		Schools in Gujarat
21	**School**	Ahmedabad International School
	Website	http://www.aischool.net/
	Tel:	91 079 26872459
22	**School**	Fountainhead School
	Website	http://www.fountainheadschools.org/
	Tel:	91 261 3103441
23	**School**	The Calorx School
	Website	http://www.thecalorxschool.org/
	Tel:	91 79 65444362
24	**School**	Navrachana International School
	Website	http://navrachana.ac.in/
	Tel:	91 265 225385
		Schools in Gurgaon
25	**School**	Amity Global School,
	Website	http://www.amity.edu/
	Tel:	91 1243240104
26	**School**	Lancers International School

	Website	http://www.lancersinternationalschool.in/
	Tel:	91 124 4171900
27	**School**	Pathways School
	Website	http://www.pathways.in/gurgaon/
	Tel:	91 11 2955-1090
28	**School**	Gurgaon, Scottish High International School
	Website	http://www.scottishigh.com/index.html,
	Tel:	91 124 4112781
29	**School**	Gurgaon, The Shri Ram School,
	Website	http://www.tsrs.org/portal/
	Tel:	91 124 4784409
		Schools in Hyderabad
30	**School**	DRS International School,
	Website	http://www.drsinternational.com/
	Tel:	91 9246550324
31	**School**	Hillside Academy
	Website	http://www.manipalhillside.com/
	Tel:	91 040 23546113
32	**School**	Indus International School, Hyderabad
	Website	http://www.indusschool.com/
	Tel:	91 8417 302100
33	**School**	International School of Hyderabad
	Website	http://www.ishyd.org/

	Tel:	91 40 30713869
34	**School**	Johnson Grammar School ICSE
	Website	http://johnsonib.com/index.php,
	Tel:	91 40 2715 0555
35	**School**	Oakridge International School
	Website	http://www.oakridgeinternational.com/
	Tel:	91 40 2004 2460
36	**School**	Silver Oaks – The School of Hyderabad
	Website	http://www.silveroaksschool.com/
	Tel:	91-040-23047777
37	**School**	Sreenidhi International School
	Website	http://www.sreenidhiinternational.com/
	Tel:	91 9848413000

Schools in Indore

38	**School**	Choithram International
	Website	http://www.choithraminternational.com/
	Tel:	91 922 959 3083
39	**School**	Delhi Public School Indore
	Website	http://www.dpsindore.org/
	Tel:	91 731-3939400

Schools in Kodaikanal

40	**School**	Kodaikanal International School
	Website	http://www.kis.in/

	Tel:	91 4542 247323
		Schools in Liluah, Howarh
41	**School**	Don Bosco School
	Website	http://www.donboscoliluah.org/
	Tel:	91 33 26551075
		Schools in Lonavala
42	**School**	The Cathedral Vidya School, Lonavala
	Website	http://cathedral-lonavala.org/
	Tel:	91 2114 282393
		Schools in Lucknow
43	**School**	St. Francis' College,
	Website	http://stfranciscollege.edu.in/
	Tel:	91 522 2623712
44	**School**	La Martiniere College
	Website	http://www.lamartinierelucknow.org/
	Tel:	91-522-2235415
		Schools in Meerut
45	**School**	St. Mary's Academy
	Website	http://stmarysmeerut.com/home.php
	Tel:	91 0121 2640838
46	**School**	Vidya Global School,
	Website	http://www.vgs.vidya.in/
	Tel:	91 121 2439192

Schools in Mumbai

47	**School**	Aditya Birla World Academy
	Website	http://www.adityabirlaworldacademy.com
	Tel:	91 22 23528400
48	**School**	Ajmera Global School
	Website	http://www.ajmeraglobalschool.com/
	Tel:	91 22 32401053
49	**School**	American School of Bombay
	Website	http://www.asbindia.org/
	Tel:	91 22 67727272
50	**School**	B.D.Somani International School
	Website	http://www.bdsint.com/
	Tel:	91 22 2218 7102
51	**School**	Aditya Birla World Academy
	Website	http://www.bisschool.com/
	Tel:	91 22 2364-8206
52	**School**	Bombay International School
	Website	http://www.bisschool.com/
	Tel:	91 22 2364-8206
53	**School**	D Y Patil International School
	Website	http://www.dypisworli.in/
	Tel:	91 22 24305555
54	**School**	Dhirubhai Ambani International School

	Website	http://www.da-is.org/
	Tel:	91 22 4061 7000
55	**School**	Dr. Pillai Global Academy
	Website	http://www.drpillaiglobalacademy.ac.in/
	Tel:	91 22 2868 4467
56	**School**	Dr. Pillai Global Academy, HOC
	Website	http://www.drpillaiglobalacademy.ac.in/
	Tel:	91 99 3022 0983
57	**School**	Dr. Pillai Global Academy, New Panvel
	Website	http://www.drpillaiglobalacademy.ac.in/
	Tel:	91 22 2522 4856
58	**School**	Ecole Mondiale World School
	Website	http://www.ecolemondiale.org/
	Tel:	91 22 2623 7265
59	**School**	Fazlani L'Académie Globale
	Website	http://www.flag.org.in/
	Tel:	91 022 32642730
60	**School**	Garodia International Centre for Learning
	Website	http://www.garodiainternational.org/
	Tel:	91 22 3263 9297
61	**School**	HFS International
	Website	http://www.hiranandanischools.edu.in/
	Tel:	91 22 2576 3001

62	**School**	HVB Global Academy
	Website	http://www.hvbglobalacademy.org/
	Tel:	91 22 61436071
63	**School**	Jamnabai Narsee School
	Website	http://www.jns.ac.in/
	Tel:	91 22 2618 7575
64	**School**	Learning Panorama School
	Website	http://panoramaschool.org/home
	Tel:	91 22 6553 9224
65	**School**	Mainadevi Bajaj International School
	Website	http://www.mbis.org.in/
	Tel:	91-22-28733807
66	**School**	NES International School Mumbai
	Website	http://www.nesinternational.org/
	Tel:	91 22 66415555
67	**School**	NSS Hill Spring International School
	Website	http://www.nsseducation.org/
	Tel:	91 22 2352 6297
68	**School**	Oberoi International School
	Website	http://www.oberoi-is.org/
	Tel:	91 22 2849 6593
69	**School**	Podar International School
	Website	http://www.podarinternationalschool.com

	Tel:	91 22 645 11109
70	**School**	Pranjali International School
	Website	http://www.pranjali.ac.in/08/The_School.html
	Tel:	91 22 2363 9166
71	**School**	RBK International Academy
	Website	http://www.rbkia.org/
	Tel:	91 22 26845666
72	**School**	Singapore International School,
	Website	http://www.sisindia.net/
	Tel:	91 2229452182
73	**School**	SVKM International School
	Website	http://ibdp.svkm.ac.in/
	Tel:	91 22 26244212
74	**School**	D Y Patil International School
	Website	http://www.dypisnerul.in/
	Tel:	91 22 47700840
		Schools in Mussoorie
75	**School**	Mussoorie International School
	Website	http://www.misindia.net/
	Tel:	91-135-2632763
76	**School**	Woodstock School
	Website	http://www.woodstockschool.in/
	Tel:	91-135-661-5000

Schools in Nagpur

77	**School**	D Y Patil International School
	Website	http://www.dypisnagpur.in/
	Tel:	91 7103 645302

Schools in Nainital

78	**School**	Birla Vidyamandir
	Website	http://www.birlavidyamandir.com/
	Tel:	91 5942 - 238729
79	**School**	Sherwood College
	Website	http://www.sherwood.edu.in/default.html
	Tel:	91-5942-239502

Schools in Nasik

80	**School**	Rasbihari International School
	Website	http://www.rasbihari.org/
	Tel:	91 253 2513622

Schools in New Delhi

81	**School**	American Embassy School
	Website	http://aes.ac.in/
	Tel:	91 11 2688 8854
82	**School**	Pathways School (NOIDA) NCR East
	Website	http://www.pathways.in/noida/
	Tel:	91 11 2955-1090
83	**School**	Pathways World School

	Website	http://www.pathways.in/#
	Tel:	91 124 231 8888
84	**School**	The British School
	Website	http://www.british-school.org/
	Tel:	91 11 2467 8524

Schools in Patna

85	**School**	Delhi Public School
	Website	http://www.dpspatna.com/
	Tel:	91 6115 225118

Schools in Pinjore

86	**School**	Delhi Public School Pinjore
	Website	http://www.dpspinjore.com/
	Tel:	91-1733-308406

Schools in Pune

87	**School**	Indus International School, Pune
	Website	http://www.indusschool.com/
	Tel:	91 02039172221
88	**School**	International School Aamby
	Website	http://www.internationalschoolaamby.com
	Tel:	91 20 3910 2512
89	**School**	Mahindra United World College of India
	Website	http://www.uwcmahindracollege.org/
	Tel:	91 20 22943262

90	**School**	Mercedes-Benz International School
	Website	http://www.mbis.org/
	Tel:	91 20 22934420
91	**School**	Sharad Pawar International School, Pune
	Website	http://www.internationalschool.in/
	Tel:	91 20 30612700
92	**School**	Symbiosis International School
	Website	symbiosisinternationalschool.net/final_site
	Tel:	91 20 2663 4550
93	**School**	Victorious Kidss Educares
	Website	http://www.victoriouskidsseducares.org/
	Tel:	91 20 26718108
94	**School**	Vishwashanti Gurukul
	Website	http://www.mitgurukul.com/
	Tel:	91 20 39210000

Schools in Rajasthan

95	**School**	Sangam School of Excellence
	Website	http://www.sangamschoolbhilwara.com/
	Tel:	91 94 14029711
96	**School**	Step by Step International School
	Website	http://www.sbshigh.net/index.shtml
	Tel:	91 992 8742 269

Schools in Rajkot

97	**School**	The Galaxy School,
	Website	http://www.tges.org/
	Tel:	91 281 2588391
		Schools in Shimla
98	**School**	Bishop Cotton School
	Website	http://www.bishopcottonshimla.com/
	Tel:	91-177-2620880
		Sohna, Haryana
99	**School**	GD Goenka World School
	Website	http://www.gdgoenka.com/gdgws/
	Tel:	91 12 4236 2895
		Nilgiris, Tamil Nadu
100	**School**	Crescent Castle Public School
	Website	www.crescentschoolooty.com/home.html
	Tel:	91 423 2443538
101	**School**	Good Shepherd International School
	Website	http://www.gsis.ac.in/
	Tel:	91 423 2550 071

Index

1

A

B

C

D

G

H

I

J

K

L

M

N

R

S

T

U

V

W

Made in the USA
San Bernardino, CA
27 December 2016